123 HOME GUIDES

VEGETABLE GARDENING

by Dixie Dean Trainer

PLAYMORE, INC. Publishers
Under arrangement with I. WALDMAN AND SON, INC.
New York, New York

For Bill

Printed in Canada.

CONTENTS

4 *Preface*
GARDENING IS A LABOR OF LOVE
And the right approach can increase
the love and reduce the labor

6 *Chapter One*
ANYONE CAN GARDEN
You don't need a green thumb
to raise vegetables

11 *Chapter Two*
YEAR ROUND MULCHING
The technique that gets rid of plowing,
hoeing, weeding and cultivating

15 *Chapter Three*
GETTING STARTED
Sun, moisure, nutrients, soil—
these are the big four

29 *Chapter Four*
PLANNING YOUR GARDEN
What are you going to plant?

40 *Chapter Five*
PREPARING YOUR GARDEN
Or, doing the spadework

45 *Chapter Six*
WHEN AND HOW TO PLANT
Including frost maps and planting times

53 *Chapter Seven*
LETTING NATURE WORK FOR YOU
How to attract birds, insects and worms,
and how to put them to work for you

57 *Chapter Eight*
HOW TO MAKE COMPOST
Homemade soil

64 *Chapter Nine*
DIRT-CHEAP GARDENING IDEAS
Great ideas for no money

68 *Chapter Ten*
GROWING A BETTER GARDEN
A plant-by-plant guide

Preface

Gardening is a labor of love, but the right approach can increase the love and reduce the labor.

This is the story of how two amateurs learned to grow vegetables successfully in Connecticut. That may seem a very limited goal indeed (although it was quite enough for us), but we did it. And if we did it, you can, too. I do think that the gardening procedures we learned about and followed will help other beginning gardeners who would like to have the pleasure of growing their own vegetables without having to spend a terrific amount of time, money, or effort.

There is effort involved in any garden, of course; there always is in a project that you consider worthwhile. But that effort was pleasurable and rewarding. What we did manage to avoid was the drudgery of gardening—the monotonous, repetitive, backbreaking jobs of weeding, hoeing, and watering. We avoided all of that by laying down a thick carpeting of hay between the rows, and let 'er rip. This is mulching, and it proved to be indispensable for us amateur and, worse than that, weekend, gardeners.

Nor did we spend a lot of time spraying various insect pests. Many of them never came to plague us anyway, thank goodness. Instead, we warded off many pests by putting in plants that would either repel them by smelling up the place (as far as bug or insect was concerned) or that would so bedazzle them that they would ignore the vegetables. The slugs took a great fancy to my marigolds one year, and chewed them to bits, but left the neighboring peppers alone.

And we didn't want to spend a lot of money on our garden. For one thing, we couldn't, and for another, it just didn't make good economic sense. We have pretty well stayed at the spade-pitchfork-rake level, although I lost my head badly last spring and bought trellis netting for the peas and cucumbers. We have tried to make do, or do without, as they say up in New England, and by and large we have succeeded.

In any case, we have managed to develop a flourishing, productive vegetable garden that has given us a great deal of pleasure—to say nothing of a great deal of squash, tomatoes, peas, beets, and onions. If we can do it, then you can, also. I hope this book will help you to achieve that goal. ●

You can put a garden anyplace, including out in the middle of a field like Lee and Dan Olsen did. An easy way to enlarge this plot each year would be to ring it with layers of newspapers in the fall to rot the surrounding sod.

This is Nancy Jarvis, with a wheel barrow load of Danver Half Long and Royal Chantenay carrots from her garden. Believe it or not, she and her husband Bill collected this harvest from seeds they had saved for several years. Bill wasn't sure they'd come up, but they "did vigorously," to put it mildly.

These little girls know a ripe tomato when they see one. . .or two. . .or three. Their grandmother, Mrs. Ben Turkek, gets the credit for the juicy fruits.

This is 7-year-old Mark Anderson, holding a cabbage that he and his brother grew in their very own garden. Now if a kid can grow a great big cabbage like that. . .

Gardens will generously repay your time and effots. Mark Anderson (left) and his big brother Christopher (right) posed for this picture in the middle of the summer when their garden was still bearing. Look what they also harvested that fall when everything was picked because of frost! They've been gardening since they were each about three years old, and although they're not crazy about the weeding and watering chores, "they certainly do enjoy the end results," as their mother put it.
Get busy, everybody!

Gurney's

Chapter One

ANYONE CAN GARDEN

You don't need

a green thumb

to raise vegetables.

Of course we would have a vegetable garden. Bill and I both wanted to feast again on rich, red tomatoes, dripping with juice and bursting with flavor. We wanted our boys to have the utterly astonishing experience of uprooting a feathery tuft of green and finding a carrot attached to the bottom. We even thought we might plant some catnip for the cat. After all, having a garden was one of the things one could do—nay, *must* do—on a piece of country property.

No matter that we were city dwellers, who could spend only weekends and school vacations tending that vegetable garden. We assumed that we could plant the seeds on a weekend, and that somehow they would have to grow during the week without further ministrations from us. After all, everything seemed to flourish on our property in Connecticut; why not vegetables? Our vision of a flourishing garden never included weeds, and, as it turned out, we never did have to contend with those.

Nor did it matter that we knew virtually nothing about growing vegetables, either from experience or from observation. What I remembered most about my parents' World War II Victory Garden was running up and down the rows of lettuce with a bushel basket, looking for rabbits to trap under it. Although Bill's practical experience was not much more than mine, he had at least observed his family's wartime gardening attempts in Bangor, Maine and had drawn some conclusions. "If tomatoes and green beans can grow in Bangor, they can grow anywhere," he said. As it turned out, he was right.

We did, however, know what we wanted to plant, or, more precisely, what we wanted to eat. Bill wanted beets for the beet greens, and bell peppers. I wanted yellow wax beans and tomatoes. Kevin asked for parsley and carrots. Colin, who was then only 4, decided he'd like carrots and some flowers.

Naturally, we told all our friends about the wonderful garden we were going to have (this was in January), and so we were soon taking orders for their favorite vegetables, too. Norma wanted eggplant, and we agreed to put in a dozen of those. (Mercifully, since we were not too crazy about eggplant, they did rather poorly that year). My mother thought we should have onions, since that was the year that the price of onions had shot through the roof, and they

This is why I suggest that you should plant what you like to eat, in this case yellow wax beans. Nature's bounty can really be staggering.

Burpee Seeds

Bush beans are a very rewarding crop to grow for the beginner. The seeds are big and easy to plant, and germinate in a week. The plants really look like something when they come out of the ground. Given half a chance, they will provide you with more beans than you can dream of. These are yellow beans, Burpee's Brittle Wax. Delicious. We like bush beans, but if you're limited for space, try the climbing varieties.

were being referred to as the "yellow diamonds of the kitchen," just as truffles were referred to as the "black diamonds of the kitchen." Another friend wanted zucchini, and still another said we should definitely plant basil, since it grew like crazy and was very easy to cultivate. We enthusiastically agreed to all suggestions. Why not? Sitting in front of the fire in January, we seemed to have unlimited space, time, and energy for everything.

I have since learned that it makes better sense to plant only those things that you really like or can't get in the stores. The main reason for planting what you like to eat is that you'll have to eat it—and probably lots of it—when the crop comes in. Given half a chance, Nature is unbelievably prolific. She, after all, is endeavoring to reproduce the species, which is the real reason for all those beans and tomatoes, which contain the seeds for the next generation. The fact that they taste good to us is just a fringe benefit. When the beans came in, seemingly all at once, we ate green beans and yellow wax beans every night for two weeks until I thought I would scream. My cousin in Litchfield, Conn. wrote at the height of the season to say that if she herself saw another bean she would assuredly be the first woman on the moon.

For somewhat different reasons, I have come to the conclusion that it makes sense not to plant vegetables that you can get easily in the stores. Now that onions have reverted to what passes for a normal price, I doubt that I will continue to plant them. I can always get good onions and scallions in the supermarkets the year round, whereas I cannot get beet greens, swiss chard, or leaf lettuce. I would rather plant these, thus making better use of our garden space, and our gardening efforts.

However, that first year we were innocent of such experiences. By February when the seed catalogs started arriving, we had quite a list of vegetables that we wanted to try. We decided to order seeds for those things that can't be transplanted, like the root vegetables, and those that can go directly into the ground early, such as lettuce. Later we would buy flats of seedlings for crops that require a long growing season, like zucchini, peppers, and tomatoes. At least their growing season was longer than the one we enjoy in Connecticut, where the last frost date in the spring is May 31 and the first frost date in the fall can occur anytime after the first week in September. That year, as a strict novice, I was not about to start raising vegetables from seed under flourescent lights in a city apartment. (Eventually I succumbed to the temptation and did just that, but that's another story).

It may seem peculiar that a gardening enthusiast can spring from the city pavements, but I believe that the enjoyment of plants which can lead to a love of gardening can develop anywhere, whether over a pot of dime-store philodendrons or in a field of Kansas corn.

Mine had begun a few years earlier on the streets of New York City, which also provided me, believe it or not, with my first garden. It was a 3' × 4' patch of dirt surrounding a newly planted tree, one of 20 such trees purchased by block residents to beautify our streets. I was thrilled to have my own little sidewalk garden, known in typically ugly bureaucratese as a "tree pit." As I dreamed of flowers and ivy foaming around the base of the tree, I suddenly realized that I didn't have the slightest idea of how to accomplish that end. I didn't know what would grow well under a tree, let alone under a tree on a city street.

That winter I ransacked the local library for books that would give me the answer. Since I didn't know exactly what to read, I read everything—books on flower gardening, vegetable gardening, and landscape gardening; books on pruning practices, evergreen shrubs, and ground covers. To my astonishment, I found I loved it all.

Fortunately, one of the first books I came across was Ruth Stout's wonderful How to Have a Green Thumb Without an Aching Back. In it she describes her early experiences as a novice gardener tending a huge place in Connecticut, to which she and her husband Fred had fled after deciding that they could not stand New York City one minute longer. (This was around in 1938, I believe).

For me, her book was absolutely engrossing, like a wonderful fairy tale. It had heroes like Fred, and John, the local farmer who owned a tractor and had Experience. It had horrible villains, like the dreaded witch grass, which can invade a garden and ruin it in a matter of weeks by choking out every other living plant in its way. It had great triumphs, like the day Ruth Stout discovered the principle of Year Round Mulching. Reading of these struggles, setbacks, and ultimate triumphs, I felt like a medieval monk breathlessly following the struggles of St. George and the Dragon.

Little did I know that in a few years I would be struggling with similar villains (including the dreaded witch grass!) in my own garden in Connecticut, not far from Ruth Stout's. In fact, I was so close that I eventually was able to visit her at the very site of her glorious encounters with nature. And there I saw what a no-work garden was all about—and how it flourished. ●

Watermelons like these are sure to make
a big hit with the small fry.

Northrup, King, Inc.

Here the Rob Zalucky family gathers the first
asparagus of the season from their
well-mulched garden.

As any devotee of (organic) gardening will tell you, Ruth Stout is a legend in her own time. It's not surprising. She is a terrifically funny, independent woman who has always charted her own zestful course through life, tweaking the beards of "experts," and thumbing her nose at pomposity and hypocrisy. Along the way she developed and promoted a splendid method of no-work gardening that took practically all the drudgery out of having a garden. It also eliminated a good deal of the expense of gardening, such as renting or buying the heavy equipment that is peddled every spring. Given a few years for the soil to improve, it made fertilizing unnecessary, except for a yearly dusting of cottonseed meal. (As our garden has not yet reached this stage, we still fertilize the tomatoes, beans and whatever else looks droopy.

Such is the stuff that legends are made of in the horticultural world.

When I realized that we were living only about 20 miles from her place, I wrote her a note asking if we could visit and see her garden. A postcard written in a firm hand arrived in the mail a few days later giving her telephone number and asking me to call to set up an appointment.

The following week, as instructed, we asked the postmaster for directions to Poverty Hollow; he just pointed to a map of the town marked with a red X. That was Ruth Stout's place.

That summer—1975—Ruth Stout was 91 years old, a bit stooped over and wearing a faded wrapper and blue felt carpet slippers. Her first question was whether I had parked the car out of sight of her sister's house. "If she sees I've got visitors, she'll come over and interrupt us," she said, "She's afraid I'll get tired out." She shook her head at the very idea, and beckoned us inside.

She was a bit long in the tooth, as they say,

Chapter Two

YEAR ROUND MULCHING

The technique that gets rid of plowing, hoeing, weeding and cultivating. All you do is plant and pick.

Burpee Seeds

Black plastic mulch speeds the growth of these Big Girl Hybrid VF tomatoes.

but all her teeth were her own; and if her white hair was not as luxuriant as it once was, well, she still had a lot of it. She used an old scuffle hoe as a staff when we went out to view her garden, but out she went, talking away and laughing in deep, rich gusts of amusement that seemed to well up from within.

We were—or at least I was—terrifically excited to meet this great lady in person; it was like visiting a national monument. And if she was somewhat less than thrilled to see us—she has, after all, been hostess to something more than 7,000 visitors over the years—she never let on. In fact, she made us feel as though we had done her an immense favor by coming to see her garden!

After we had had a nice, long talk, she took me out through an opening in a great hedge of lilacs to see her world-famous garden. It was fenced around with chicken wire and saplings, along which grew cucumbers and squash, as I recall. In the middle was an enormous 10′ high cage roofed and sided with chicken wire. The cage is not to keep anything in; it is to keep

raccoons out of her sweet corn. I remembered that she had told in one of her books how she had inveigled her brother Rex Stout, the novelist, into building this very successful contraption for her.

And all in between the plants, wherever one looked, carpeting the whole of the fenced-in garden, was hay. Hay in all stages of being hay. Light, tawny hay, newly put down; walnut colored hay that had darkened under exposure to sun and rain; rotted down hay that seemed to be sinking blackly into the black earth. In fact, it was hard to tell where hay and earth separated.

And that was the point of the whole system. The remarkable, revolutionary idea that Ruth Stout has been espousing all these years is, very simply, *year round mulching with hay*. This undoubtedly sounds like jabberwock if you are unfamiliar with the idea. Indeed, it took me several readings and rereadings of her books until the concept finally made sense. Then I found myself saying, "Aha! So *that's* how it works."

And it does work. In fact, it does most of the

work of gardening—the drudgery—for you. This past August I actually found myself wondering if there wasn't something I could *do* in the garden besides harvesting the crops. There wasn't.

To explain year round mulching with hay, let me begin at the beginning.

A *mulch* is a covering spread over the ground to perform one or more of several functions. A mulch can keep the ground beneath moist by slowing down evaporation. It can prevent the growth of weeds by denying them light and air. It can insulate the plant from heat or cold, and can provide a soft, dirt-free place where fruits and vegetables can mature without resting on the ground (a leading cause of spots and rots). It can fertilize the soil as it decomposes.

People use many different materials for mulches: hay, salt hay, pine bark chips, peanut hulls, leaves, grass clippings, seaweed, newspapers, and even stones. (The latter popular in Japan and New England), it would seem.) Black plastic has been highly touted and is widely used as a mulch. I personally don't like the looks or feel of it, so I have never tried it, but there are those who swear by it.

Year round mulching is just that. Once you spread the mulch-hay over the garden patch, you leave it there. It will gradually decompose, adding richness to the soil. You don't have to do anything to it. That is, you don't have to work at it—no forking it over, or digging it into the soil, or rolling it up at the end of the season. Just leave it, and let nature do the work for you.

In the spring, you will probably want to spread more hay over the stuff that's already there—partly to replenish the mulch and partly for looks. In the fall, if you get around to it, you can spread some leaves over the hay (purists don't), and then put another light blanket of hay over the area. Doing this makes me feel as though I'm tucking the garden in for the winter.

Once you get used to the idea of it, a garden mulched with hay also looks nice. The sight of an unmulched garden, with bare earth packed down between the rows of plants, fills me with sadness. I feel sorry for the poor plants, gasping as they are under the hot summer sun; and I feel even sorrier for the owner, who must have to do such a tremendous amount of work to keep the aisles clear, as it were.

Year round mulching with hay. And you use hay. Why hay? Well, for one thing it's cheap. You don't use fancy hay that's used for feeding livestock; you ask for spoiled or mulch hay, which the farmer can't feed to his animals. In our area of Connecticut, a bale of mulch hay now sells for $12.50, which I don't exactly consider cheap, but that's the going price. It is, however, a lot cheaper than mulches like wood chips or pine bark, which would only cover about a third of the area at about three times the cost.

Hay is also usually readily available, unless you happen to live in the middle of a large city, in which case you probably don't have much room for a garden anyway. (In that case, a mulch of pine bark chips would probably do fine). If you are short on local farmers, try a riding stable.

Hay has other attributes. It looks nice, it smells nice, and it feels nice underfoot. When you first pile it on, you will have great fluffy mounds of golden straw between your planting rows, but they will quickly flatten down under the pressure of foot traffic and rains. This very fluffiness means that the hay won't pack down solidly, so that rain will continue to pass right through and into the earth and so on down to the plant's roots. Leaves can form a dense, impenetrable mat that will prevent any moisture from seeping through. Black plastic, of course, forms an impenetrable barrier to rain.

Hay also decomposes gradually, adding richness and texture to the soil as it does so.

What all this means is that for the price of a couple of bales of hay, you will at one stroke eliminate the jobs of: plowing, weeding, hoeing, cultivating, fertilizing and watering (and worrying about doing all of the above).

As Ruth Stout told me, "With my system, all you have to is plant 'em and pick 'em." By and large, she was right.

Until you get started, it seems an odd system. Here are some common questions and answers about year round mulching with hay.

1. When do you put on the hay mulch?

When you start planting in the spring. After you get your seeds or seedlings in, spread the hay in between the planting rows, bringing it up as close as you can to the furrow. In the case of big seeds like beans and peas, you can actually pull the hay lightly across the furrow; the coarse plants will come up through it. For the finer seeds, wait until they've germinated and you can see the tiny plants before pulling the mulch closer.

2. How thickly should you apply the hay?

Thicker than you think. I started off by putting down about two or three inches of hay, which packed down nicely. But it wasn't thick enough to keep the weeds down, so I had to add more. I didn't mind; it's not such a big job to strew handfuls of hay along a path. Ruth Stout says to put down six to eight inches of hay right off the bat and not to worry. The mountains of hay won't topple into the planting rows and smother the seedlings.

3. How does the hay keep weeds down?

Like any mulch, it prevents light and moisture from reaching the seeds and so prevents them from germinating. If a weed does pop up, you can yank it out easily because it won't be able to develop such a strong toehold—or root-hold—as a weed left to its own devices in a bare patch of garden. If you don't want to pull it out, you can throw a few more handfuls of hay on top of it. That will usually smother it for good.

In general, if you see any weeds, add more hay. You can tuck it under the plants if necessary.

4. Why don't the weed seeds in the hay germinate?

For the same reason that the weed seeds in the ground don't sprout; the hay smothers their growth. Remember, the weeds cannot grow where your vegetables are growing, for the simple reason that two bodies cannot occupy the same space at the same time. They can only grow in between the plants—in the rows, in between the tomatoes, amongst the squash. If you fill all these spots with hay, then weeds cannot grow there.

5. Do you really not have to water?

You really don't—*if* you put on a thick enough cover of hay. Last year we started another garden in a very hot sun pocket where everything grew like mad. Since it was out of the question to water this new plot, I piled on hay with a lavish hand. The soil never dried out, despite the fact we had little rain. The squash and sugar baby watermelons did quite well. Some of the tomatoes however, suffered from blossom end rot, a condition caused by the unequal absorption of water by the plant. That may have been due to the fact that I didn't water or because they were in a rough, first year garden.

By contrast, I made a mistake in the salad garden just off the deck and within easy reach of the hose. There I didn't put on as much hay as I should have, and the plants became noticeably droopy. So we had to water, which is no fun even with one of those sprinkler gadgets that fit onto the end of the hose. Next year, more hay.

6. What about cultivating? I am ashamed to say that I had to look up the meaning of this term in the dictionary, so you can see that I have never done it. Cultivating means "to loosen or break up the soil (about growing plants)." Mostly you have to do this with a hoe, or one of those garden cultivators and it seems to me like a lot of hard work. Mulching keeps the soil loose and moist so that it does not form a hard crust of earth or clumps of dirt that have to be broken up.

7. What do you do with the hay in the fall?

You leave it lying on the ground to do its stuff. The lower layer will gradually rot into the ground, enriching the soil as it does. Some people recommend that you pull up all the dead plants and put them on the compost heap. I did that with some, but some I just left in the ground and some I pulled up and laid them down on the top of the hay to rot along with the rest. (Any diseased plants should be destroyed. This kind of simple crop sanitation can forestall a lot of insects.) I put some leaves over some of the hay just because I didn't know what else to do with them. In the spring I will cover the whole works with another layer of fresh, spoiled hay.

8. How do you get started again in the spring?

This proved to be the biggest stumbling block for me. I had always heard that in the spring you had to "spade up the garden," or "turn over the soil," or plow. This seemed to be an awful lot of work to begin with. It also seemed to require pulling off all that hay that you had put on in the first place. It didn't make sense.

I finally realized that one of the major benefits of mulching is that you don't have to spade up the entire garden every spring. When you are ready to plant, all you do is rake or pull the mulch back on itself, opening up a clear lane of dirt. If you are going to plant established seedlings, you don't even have to clear a whole furrow. Just open up a clear patch about the size of a saucer and pop your plants in. Some people even plant big seeds, like corn, right through the mulch.

Why don't you have to plow? Because the ground underneath the mulch will have remained light, loose, friable and damp. The purpose of plowing or spading is to loosen up and aerate the soil. A permanent hay mulch keeps it loose and aerated.

If you want to add soil nutrients, add them directly to the cleared patches and work them into the soil. When you stop to think of it, there really isn't too much point to spading up and fertilizing the garden paths.

Suppose you want the ground to warm up quickly so that you can put in an early crop such as peas. Open up your planting rows about a week before you want to plant, and the sun will warm up the ground for you.

Once everything has been planted, you simply spread additional hay around and between the plants as you did in step one, and the cycle will repeat itself.

That's all there is to it. If you'd like to find out more and more about mulching, I heartily recommend Ruth Stout's "No Work Gardening," which is available in paperback. ●

You can make a garden—that is, you can grow vegetables—almost anywhere you please. I grew tomatoes and green peppers along the front of the house the first summer because the foundation plantings looked so scrawny. The plants, in their sunny location, rewarded us with plenty of vegetables and mountains of cooling green foliage.

Indeed, people seem to be putting in vegetable gardens in all sorts of places and making them in all sorts of shapes. There are free form gardens and individual "postage stamp" gardens that measure just 4 feet by 4 feet. Some people use parsley as a handsome border for their flowerbeds. Others grow vegetables for their ornamental value. Eggplants, for instance, were once grown mainly as ornamentals. Their light silvery green leaves contrast beautifully with much of the darker green of other plants, and they produce beautiful lavender blossoms with yellow centers.

Still in all, the regular rectangular garden plot will probably remain the hands down favorite because it is so easy to work with. The U.S. Department of Agriculture recommends "a plot near your home in full sunlight as the most convenient spot for a home vegetable garden." Unfortunately, that is also usually the most convenient spot for swings, badminton courts, or chaise lounges. So you may have to look elsewhere on your property for a garden site.

As you are looking, keep the following requirements in mind, for these are what your plants will need to reward you with an early and abundant harvest.

SUNLIGHT

Vegetables must have at least six hours of sun a day to flourish and produce fruit. That's the minimum. If you can put them in full sun, they'll do even better.

Some leafy crops, like lettuce and swiss chard, can tolerate part shade, but no amount of fertilizer, water or care can replace the needed sunshine for your other crops. You can turn a lightly shaded spot to your advantage by putting leafy crops there. I found that my lettuce lasted much longer when I put it at the bottom

Chapter Three

GETTING STARTED

Sun, moisture, nutrients, soil

—these are the big four.

How do you get them?

of the garden where it was sheltered from the late afternoon sun.

Providing adequate sunlight for your plants brings up an important pointer when you are planning your garden. Lay out your garden from north to south, with the tall plants at the north end so that they don't shade the short ones at the south.

MOISTURE

No matter what, your vegetables will need water, whether it is supplied from above by the powers that be or by you with a hose. If you mulch heavily—and again I recommend hay—you will rarely have to water your garden unless you are hit with a long dry spell.

The key thing about watering, I am told, is to water deeply or not at all. Watering deeply and well encourages the roots to go deeper and deeper into the ground where they will encounter natural moisture in the soil. If you give the garden just a top sprinkling, you'll encourage the delicate feeder roots to the surface for their water supply. There they will run the risk of being scorched by the sun if they are not protected by a hay mulch.

Some people say that the easiest way to water a garden is to set up the lawn sprinkler in the middle of the garden and let it run all night. This is okey if the sprinkler reaches all parts of your garden; otherwise you may have to go rushing out at 3. a.m. to move the sprinkler around. If you mulch you won't have to do this.

In my experience, I have found that letting the sprinker run for about an hour—*maximum*—in the cool of early evening is plenty enough. I have had to do that only a few times when we had more than a week without any rain in the middle of summer. Having the hay mulch kept the ground beneath damp until it finally saw fit to rain.

Naturally enough, too much water is just as bad as too little. When you are making your inspection tour looking for prospective garden sites, keep in mind the drainage problem. Poor drainage is indicated by where you see puddles of water collecting after a rainstorm.

NUTRIENTS

Just like the rest of us, vegetables need plenty of nutrients in order to grow, produce big yields, and early crops. A garden that has been worked for several years gradually builds up reserves of many of these nutrients from natural sources: decomposing vegetable matter and hay; perhaps wood ashes from the fireplace; and even nitrogen added to the soil by crops like peas.

For the beginner, however, faced with making a growing garden from a former weed patch or swatch of lawn, the question is: what can you do for me right now?

The first year we did a little bit of everything. We could tell that our soil was probably acid from the types of trees and bushes that grew naturally on our property—oaks, hemlocks, birch, and mountain laurel. To sweeten the soil, we covered the garden with a light dusting of lime. Our soil was on the heavy side, so we spread peat moss on top of the lime. Since there was a large plastic sack of wood ashes sitting in the closet, we added those, too as a source of potassium. And just to be on the safe side, we sprinkled an all purpose vegetable fertilizer on top of that. Then Bill turned it all under with a pitchfork.

For a first year garden, ours did pretty well. After everything was planted, we mulched with hay and sat back to wait for the results. We had more beans than we could eat, plenty of squash and a good crop of tomatoes. The beets provided us with lots of beet greens, but the beet roots themselves did not do so well. Neither did the carrots or the radishes. Later we found out that poor root crops are a common problem in first year gardens. The reason is that the soil is still too coarse and lumpy for them to grow well: it needs a few years of being worked to develop a fine texture. The peas were really a loss; we got only a cupful from a 20' row.

Basically, we were on the right track, but we could have done more. This leads right into the question of using fertilizers, a highly emotional topic (believe it or not) that splits people into two camps.

On the one hand are the believers in chemical fertilizers—the kind that you can buy in the local garden center or through a seed catalog. On the other are organic gardeners, who believe in using only non-chemical fertilizers, such as animal manure, bone meal, wood ashes, and the like.

Emotionally, I belong to the camp of organic gardeners or fertilizers. I can get wood ashes for free, cow manure for very little (there is rumored to be an elderly lady nearby who sells cow manure in three forms: fresh, dried, or frozen), and bone meal almost anyplace. I also feel that it is wasteful to use the world's resources to manufacture chemicals to use in place of natural fertilizers that already exist.

Practically speaking, I confess that I have experimented with some chemical fertilizers. I could not resist one of the "special tomato growing formulas" put out by one of the mail

Here Rev. Milton Houts of Galva, Iowa, demonstrates what good soil tilth is.

order seed companies, and it seemed to produce good results. At least we had more tomatoes than we could consume, freeze, or make into sauce. And after our miserable one-cup pea harvest, I decided to experiment with something called a "pea and bean inoculant," a topical fertilizer that is supposed to give them a big boost. You roll them around in it at planting time. It helps the peas and beans "form nodules that take nitrogen from the air and enrich the soil," to quote from the catalog of Joseph Harris, from whom I bought both peas and inoculant. I followed instructions, planted the peas in an even *worse* first year garden, and they grew like crazy. We harvested more than 20 pounds of peas from the four rows.

(After writing this, I decided it would be wise to check it out with Harris Seeds. Their very nice letter said, in part, "I was interested to learn of your success with the innoculant. Strictly speaking, this is not a fertilizer at all. It consists of live bacteria which help the legumes to form nodules on the roots, and these are what provide the nitrogen to the soil.")

And what would I advocate? For what it is worth, I will come down firmly straddling the fence and say "both." I have had good results from both, whichever seemed the most practical and/or interesting at the time.

If I can recommend anything, it's to use your common sense. Enjoy yourself. In a garden you are free to experiment and to try something new. If you want to put peppers in front of the house, go ahead and do it. It's not a lifetime decision. You can always transplant them, or cut them down, or just not put them there next year. They'll only be there for a few months, anyway.

By the same token, if you want to try out different methods of fertilizing your crops, go ahead and do it. Bury a fish head under the corn like the Indians did if you feel like it; or buy a bag of commercial fertilizer and add that to the soil if that appeals to you. (Just be sure to read the directions and don't use too much). It's your garden, so don't let the "experts" from either side intimidate you. Learn as much as you can from them, but also learn from your garden. Observe the results and see what works for you. It's helpful to keep a notebook so that you will remember because otherwise you will forget what you have done. Next year you can adjust, amplify, or eliminate certain practices.

SOIL

Of course it does help to have some idea of what it is that you are trying to accomplish by enriching your soil. Your goal is to create dirt, but dirt of such fineness, richness, and lightness that it ranks at the very pinnacle of dirtdom. This marvel of nature, this Cinderella of soil, is loam, the rich, black earth that man has always coveted (and fought wars for) because it is so productive. Not everyone is blessed with it, but it is possible to develop it.

What is loam? Loam is one of three basic

Gurney's

types of soil, the poor relations being clay and sandy soils. Loam has "good tilth," which means that it is loose and crumbly to the depth of at least one foot before your spade hits stones, shale, or clay clods. It is a soil that drains well, contains plenty of nutrients, and usually teems with beneficial earthworms. Vegetables love it.

Clay and sandy soils do not have good tilth, to put it mildly. Clay soil is made up of tiny, microscopic particles that are extremely close together. It absorbs water slowly, and holds it. A friend who is a talented potter and determined gardener told me that the soil in her garden near Philadelphia is so clay-ey that she can practically throw it on her potter's wheel. Clay soils tend to glue themselves together during wet spells so that plant roots simply cannot

Although spinach thrives in any reasonably good garden soil, it requires plenty of nitrogen. A good plan is to dig in a heavy layer of mature compost where the plants are to stand.

penetrate freely to absorb water and nutrients. Clay soils are heavy, cold, and prone to baking and crusting in summer.

Sandy soils on the other hand, have a very light, loose texture. Although air can penetrate deeply, that same looseness means that water can run right through the soil. Which it does, carrying moisture and nutrients right past the plant roots.

Loam is in the middle. It contains both clay and sand but also has a good supply of decomposed organic material—leaves, old plants, rotted wood—called humus. As a result, the grains of the soil have good structure, neither too heavy nor too light. The soil drains well, yet retains enough water for plant growth. Air can circulate, and the loose friable soil provides plenty of room for roots to grow easily.

To turn clay or sandy soils into loam fortunately does not require the skills of an alchemist. It does require some muscle, at least in the beginning. Your first job will be to build up the physical attributes of your soil so that it has "good tilth," the second will be to add various nutrients for the delectation of your plants.

Whether your soil is clay or sand, you improve it the same way: by adding compost (from your compost heap) and/or peat moss (from your garden center). Compost is partly or fully decayed vegetable matter that really adds life to your soil. It's not hard to make, especially if you are patient and let nature do the work for you. Ruth Stout says that she doesn't bother with composting because she uses everything as a mulch, and there is a lot to be said for that approach, too. She also has been enriching her garden for some four decades. Mostly I mulch, but I have found that having a small compost pile where vegetable peelings, leaves, and plant refuse can peacefully rot down together without any attention from me has been very useful. Another of compost's many virtues (this is also a subject that arouses much passion in gardening circles) is that you can make it in any quantity that you want. It will also be there when you want it, so you can add some to your plants when the spirit moves you. There are many ways of composting, and we'll get into the whole subject in detail in a later chapter.

If you don't as yet have a ready supply of compost, you can substitute peat moss, which is sold in bales at all garden centers in the spring. An enormous bale of peat moss costs about $5.00. Peat moss, as it comes out of the bale, is light, fluffy stuff that will lighten a heavy soil like clay. Once it's wet, it has great moisture retention capabilities, which makes it wonderful in a light, sandy soil.

The only problem with using it is getting it wet. If it is not wet, it will repel moisture like a sheet of plastic. I used to keep our bales of peat moss stored neatly under the deck of the house, and moisten individual buckets of it with the hose. This is about the hardest, most time consuming method possible of wetting down peat moss. I finally learned the easy way: open the bag and put it out in the open for a week. A few good spring rains will do the job for you.

The next item you should add—if you can get it—is animal manure, which acts as both a soil conditioner (because of the strawy parts) and a fertilizer (adds lots of nitrogen).

In case you didn't know, all manure is not the same. In addition to fresh, dried, and frozen, there is rotted and fresh. You should try to get rotted manure to put into your garden. The bacteria in your soil will need extra nitrogen to break down fresh manure, and this will snitch some of the nitrogen from your plants. Also, manure that has rotted or decomposed somewhat is in a form that your plants can use more easily.

The way to make rotted manure is to get a pile of it, cover it with dirt so it doesn't smell, and let it sit for a couple of months. If you don't want it in your back yard, try making a deal with a stable or dairy farmer. I know of one fellow who has the local stable make a big pile of manure for him in December; when he comes to haul it away in March, it's rotted down just right.

We made a similar deal with a dairy farmer, but got him to bring it over. I never thought I would live to see the day when I would be ecstatic to have a load of manure dumped in my backyard, but I was. That's just one of the ways that gardening changed my outlook on life.

There is more to this. You should also know that hen, horse, sheep, and rabbit manures are known as "hot" manures because of their high nitrogen content. Cow and hog manures are known as "cold" manures because they are fairly wet, low in nitrogen, and break down relatively slowly. We use cow manure because that's what we can get.

You can also buy dried manure, powdered and odorless, in sacks at your local garden center or nursery. You can work it directly into the ground.

When you have incorporated any or all of these soil conditioners into your garden, you will be amazed by the improved appearance of your soil. That is, you will be if you have added enough. Your dirt will be darker. It will be richer looking. It may even have good tilth. You are on your way to loam.

Next you must add soil nutrients. Although compost and animal manure contain some nutrients, they don't have enough for a really vig-

Soil testing kits, such as these from Sudbury Laboratories, can tell you what your soil needs and how you can correct any deficiencies. Beginners' kits will make about 70 tests—the super model will enable you to do about 260 individusal tests.

Note the warty skins on these cucumbers.
They'll make good pickles, of whatever
size you'd like to feature.

orous vegetable garden.

To survive and flourish, plants need 16 different nutrients. The major nutrients are Nitrogen (N), Phosphorus (P), and Potassium (K), about which more anon. There are also a number of minor and trace elements, including calcium, zinc, iron, manganese, sulfer, copper, and magnesium.

The Big Three—Nitrogen, Phosphorus, and Potassium—are always listed in that order on every package of fertilizer you see. For instance, the label on Hyponex, a general house plant food, reads 7-6-19, which means that it contains, respectively, 7 per cent nitrogen, 6 per cent phosphorous, and 19 per cent potassium. There are different formulations for different purposes and different plants: Ra-Pid-Grow, a popular leaf fertilizer that you spray on your plants, has for its formula 23-19-17; whereas my African violets thrive on Peter Special Violet Food, with its formula of 12-36-14. Ra-Pid-Grow has the Big Three in fairly balanced proportions; but the African violet formula has three times as much phosphorus as Nitrogen or Potassium. At first I thought those numbers of the fertilizer represented an uncrackable code; I now try to remember the order of the Big Three by the mnemonic device of No Pink Knees, which doesn't make much sense, but does help me to remember Nitrogen (N), Phosphorus (P), and Potassium (K).

How can you tell how much and what your garden needs? One way is to have your soil tested. You can send a soil sample to the local county agent of the Department of Agriculture or to the Agricultural Extension Service of your State University. They will analyze your sample for free, and tell you what it needs. Look for them (and it may take a while to find them) in the white pages of your telephone book.

Another way is to buy a soil testing kit and do it yourself. You can get these at most nurseries and garden centers or through many of the seed catalogs. Burpee's, for instance, carries what seems to be the full line of the Sudbury Soil Testing Kits. The beginner's version will make up to 70 tests and costs $8.25. (The super Deluxe model goes for $49.95 and makes about 260 individual tests). The kits come with instructions telling you how to run the tests, what the results mean, and what you should do to correct any deficiencies.

I should say a word here about the pH level in your soil, which is an indicator of whether your soil is sour (acid) or sweet (alkaline). The pH scale runs from 0 for extremely acid to 7 for neutral and on up to 14 for extremely alkaline. Most vegetables prefer soils that are neutral or slightly acid, that is, with a pH of 6.5 to 7.0

To save space, cucumbers should be trained to grow up in the air on a post or trellis.   Northrup, King, Inc.

(Tubers and root crops, including potatoes, beets, carrots and turnips like a sweeter soil.) More on that later.

You can find out this information by testing your soil, asking a gardening neighbor, or as we did, simply by observing what grows naturally around you. We looked around and it was quite apparent that our soil is on the acid side. We added lime to sweeten the soil at a rate of 5 pounds per 100 square feet.

Which brings us to the subject of adding soil nutrients, or finding sources for the Big Three, N, P, and K.

Nitrogen. Animal manures, in all their wondrous varieties, add nitrogen to the soil. So do legumes, like peas and beans, planting a few rows of them is a most painless way to improve your soil. Some other good sources of nitrogen are: Blood meal, Milorganite, Cottonseed Meal, and Fish Emulsion.

Bloodmeal, which you can buy at most nurseries, contains up to 15 per cent nitrogen and usually some phosphorous and potassium. It is also supposed to be great for scaring rabbits away from the garden patch—one whiff of blood meal and they're off to the neighbors.

Milorganite is the trade name for activated sewage sludge that is processed and sold by many cities to make money and recycle municipal wastes. Milorganite is odorless, contains up to 6 per cent nitrogen, and can be found in nurseries.

Cottonseed meal, Ruth Stout's favorite, contains about 7 per cent nitrogen. She applies it at a rate of 1 pound per 100 square feet, using for measuring sticks two 10 feet saplings that she lays out at right angles to each other.

Fish emulsion has 5 to 10 per cent nitrogen, and is often used as a "booster" feeding midway through the season when the plants, especially the heavy feeders, can use a shot in the arm, as it were.

Phosphorus. The best source of phosphorus is Bone Meal, available at any garden supply store. It contains a huge amount of phosphoric acid—20 to 25 per cent or more—as well as 1 to 2 per cent nitrogen. Vegetables love it, and if you have any left over, so will your daffodils and tulips.

Some gardeners use rock phosphate or superphosphate instead of bone meal. This is a finely ground rock powder, containing up to 30 per cent phosphoric acid.

Potassium. The best natural source for potassium is wood ashes, the common wood ashes right out of your fireplace. Most wood ash contains 7 to 8 per cent potassium, and is free for the burning. Putting the wood ashes back into the ground is, I think, a fitting end for a tree.

Two years ago we had two swamp maples cut down because they were choking out a really handsome stand of hemlocks near the house. The maples were typical second growth trees—on a crowded woodlot—tall and skinny with bushy tops reaching for the light. The man who cut them down sawed the trunks into logs for the fireplace, and then asked if we wanted him to haul the bushy tops off to the dump. We said no, and for one year had a rather unsightly brush pile. The following year when it was nice and dry, we spent a couple of fall afternoons breaking up the brush into kindling, and we used it in fires that winter. In the spring we spread the wood ashes from the fires over the garden.

Those swamp maples were useful from the beginning to the end. In their early days they provided shade and shelter; cut down, they became a source of heat and light; and at the end they returned to replenish and enrich the earth.

If you have trees around your house, you probably have a source of wood ashes you've overlooked (without cutting down a thing). Trees naturally shed dead branches and limbs over the winter, so when you go around cleaning up this debris in the spring, don't throw all those sticks into the trash. Turn them into wood ashes. If you haven't got a fireplace, you can make a nice little fire on your barbecue grill and toast hot dogs while you're at it. You'll feed your stomach and your garden at the same time.

Incidentally, store your wood ashes in a dry place until you are ready to put them in the garden at planting time. If you leave them outdoors in the rain and snow, most of the potassium will be leached away by the water. We keep ours in old plastic bags inside cardboard grocery cartons.

To put the Big Three in your garden, You can, of course, use a chemical fertilizer or fertilizers (as in the case of special formulas for tomatoes). There are many different products on the market, so be sure to read the labels carefully and follow directions accurately. Too much of a good thing in the way of chemical fertilizers can kill your plants.

As the USDA points out in its bulletin called "Growing Vegetables," "However, failure to bear fruit and even injury to the plants may result from the use of too much plant nutrient, particularly chemical fertilizers, or from an unbalanced nutrient condition in the soil. Because of the small quanitities of fertilizer required for short rows and small plots it is easy to apply too much fertilizer." The USDA recommends always weighing or measuring your fertilizer accurately before applying.

A gardener who designed a vegetable garden for a woman's magazine had this advice: "The best type is a special vegetable fertilizer that releases nitrogen slowly and can be applied at planting time. Other fertilizers may release nitrogen too rapidly, so they have to be applied up to two weeks ahead of plantings to prevent burning the young seedlings."

The first year, when we put everything we could lay our hands on in the garden patch, we used a general all purpose vegetable fertilizer, on the theory that "it couldn't hurt." I'm not so sure that I would do that again. I feel that mulching and using whatever natural fertilizers we can get are preferable. However, Bill wants to add more chemical fertilizers to the garden this year, so I suppose we will compromise in some fashion. We may wind up adding fertilizer to one section, leaving one alone except for additional hay mulch, and adding wood ashes and bone meal and cottonseed meal to another section.

In any event, as I write this on a cold January afternoon, the actual working in the garden seems far off. And thank goodness for that. Right now all we can do is to plan our garden, doing nothing more strenuous than lifting a pencil and turning the pages of the seed catalogs as we dream great dreams of summer's bounty. ●

AGRICULTURAL COLLEGES AND
OFFICES OF AGRICULTURAL EXTENSION SERVICES

Thanks to our farming forebearers, all land-grant universities must have an Agricultural College and provide free information on agriculture to the citizenry. That's us.

As a result, you will find that you can get a great deal of free information and advice just for the asking. The state agricultural extension service offices can provide you with lists of recommended varieties that have proved successful in your area. They have information compiled from tests on various pesticides and fertilizers. They can either test your soil for free for you, or they will tell you where to send it. Write, call, or pay them a visit. You'll enjoy it.

Agricultural Information
Auburn University
Auburn, ALABAMA 36830

Agricultural Information
University of Alaska
College, ALASKA 99701

Agricultural Information
College of Agriculture
University of Arizona
Tucson, ARIZONA 85721

Agricultural Information
University of Arkansas
Box 391
Little Rock,
ARKANSAS 72203

Agricultural Information
Agricultural Extension Service
200 University Avenue
Berkeley,
CALIFORNIA 94720

Agricultural Information
Colorado State University
Fort Collins,
COLORADO 80521

Agricultural Information
College of Agriculture
University of Connecticut
Storrs,
CONNECTICUT 06268

Agricultural Information
College of Agricultural
  Sciences
University of Delaware
Newark, DELAWARE 19711

Agricultural Information
University of Florida
217 Rolfs Hall
Gainesville, FLORIDA 32601

Agricultural Information
College of Agriculture
University of Georgia
Athens, GEORGIA 30602

Agricultural Information
University of Hawaii
2500 Dole St.
Honolulu, HAWAII 96822

Agricultural Information
College of Agriculture
University of Idaho
Moscow, IDAHO 83843

Agricultural Information
College of Agriculture
University of Illinois
Urbana, ILLINOIS 61801

Agricultural Information
Agricultural Administration
  Bldg.
Purdue University
Lafayette, INDIANA 47907

Agricultural Information
Iowa State University
Ames, IOWA 50010

Agricultural Information
Kansas State University
Manhattan, KANSAS 66502

Agricultural Information
College of Agriculture
University of Kentucky
Lexington,
KENTUCKY 40506

Agricultural Information
Louisiana State University
Knapp Hall, University Station
Baton Rouge,
LOUISIANA 70803

Agricultural Information
Department of Public
  Information
University of Maine
Orono, MAINE 04473

Agricultural Information
University of Maryland
Agricultural Division
College Park,
MARYLAND 20742

Agricultural Information
Stockbridge Hall
University of Massachusetts
Amherst,
MASSACHUSETTS 01002

Agricultural Information
Department of Information
  Services
109 Agricultural Hall
East Lansing,
MICHIGAN 48823

Department of Information
Institute of Agriculture
University of Minnesota
St. Paul, MINNESOTA 55101

Agricultural Information
Mississippi State University
State College,
MISSISSIPPI 39762

Agricultural Information
1-98 Agricultural Building
University of Missouri
Columbia, MISSOURI 65201

Office of Information
Montana State University
Bozeman,
MONTANA 59715

Department of Information
College of Agriculture
University of Nebraska
Lincoln, NEBRASKA 68503

Agricultural Communications
  Service
University of Nevada
Reno, NEVADA 89507

Agricultural Information
Schofield Hall
University of
  New Hampshire
Durham,
NEW HAMPSHIRE 03824

Agricultural Information
College of Agriculture
Rutgers—The State
  University
New Brunswick,
NEW JERSEY 08903

Agricultural Information
Drawer 3A1
New Mexico State University
Las Cruces,
NEW MEXICO 88001

Agricultural Information
State College of Agriculture
Cornell University
Ithaca, NEW YORK 14850

Agricultural Information
North Caroline State
  University
State College Station
Raleigh, NORTH
CAROLINA 27607

Agricultural Information
North Dakota State University
State University Station
Fargo,
NORTH DAKOTA 58102

Cooperative Extension
  Service
The Ohio State University
2120 Fyffe Road
Columbus, OHIO 43210

Agricultural Information
Oklahoma State University
Stillwater,
OKLAHOMA 74704

Agricultural Information
206 Waldo Hall
Oregon State University
Corvallis, OREGON 97331

Agricultural Information
The Pennsylvania State
  University
Room 1, Armsby Building
University Park,
PENNSYLVANIA 16802

Cooperative Extension Service
University of Puerto Rico
Mayaguez Campus, Box AR
Rio Piedras,
PUERTO RICO 00928

Agricultural Information
University of Rhode Island
16 Woodwall Hall
Kingston,
RHODE ISLAND 02881

Agricultural Information
Clemson University
Clemson,
SOUTH CAROLINA 29631

Agricultural Information
South Dakota State University
University Station
Brookings,
SOUTH DAKOTA 57006

Agricultural Information
University of Tennessee
Box 1071
Knoxville,
TENNESSEE 37901

Department of Agricultural
  Information
Services Building
Texas A&M University
College Station, TEXAS 77843

Agricultural Information
Utah State University
Logan, UTAH 84321

Agricultural Information
University of Vermont
Burlington, VERMONT 05401

Agricultural Information
Virginia Polytechnic
  Institute
Blacksburg, VIRGINIA 24061

Agricultural Information
115 Wilson Hall
Washington State University
Pullman,
WASHINGTON 99163

Agricultural Information
Evansdale Campus
Appalachian Center
West Virginia University
Morgantown,
WEST VIRGINIA 26506

Agricultural Information
University of Wisconsin
Madison, WISCONSIN 53706

Agricultural Information
University of Wyoming
Box 3354
Laramie, WYOMING 82070

Information Services
Federal Extension Service
U.S. Department of
  Agriculture
WASHINGTON, D.C. 20250

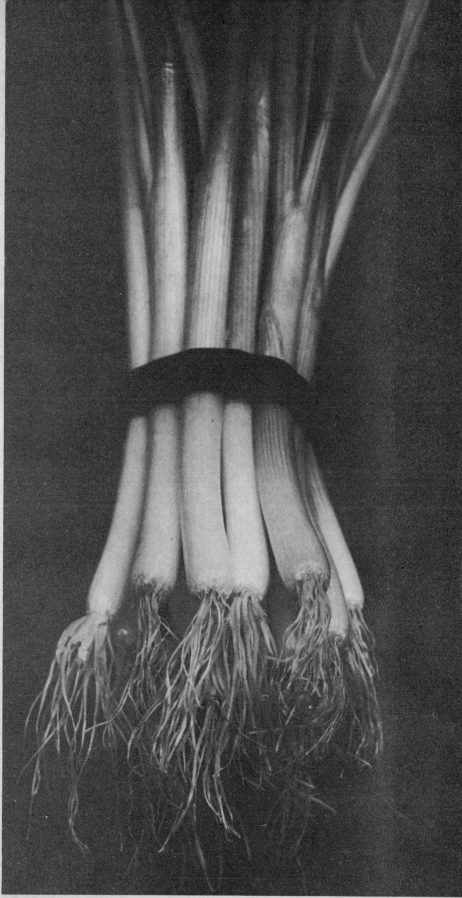

Onions are a deservedly popular
crop with many gardeners.

Chapter Four

In gardening, as in many other endeavors, advance planning is the key to success. Without a thought-out garden plan, you may find yourself, as I once did, standing in the garden with a fistful of seed packets, wondering where to put what. Back to the drawing boards.

Planning a garden is a lot of fun, although it can get complicated as you start figuring out all the variations, which can be quite elegant and challenging. What you'll need is lots of paper, some pencils, a selection of seed catalogs, and plenty of time. I like to plan next year's garden while sitting comfortably in front of a blazing fire while the February winds howl outside. I can make endless lists and shift things around a lot, because it's a simple task to move a row of carrots on paper. Once they're in the ground it's a different matter.

Start by asking yourself how big a garden you want to have. It is much, much better to have a small garden that you can take care of easily than a big one that will overwhelm you. You'll have much more pleasure from a smaller one and probably a bigger harvest, since you'll have time to pamper your plants. A good size for beginner gardeners seems to be around 200 square feet. Our first one measured about 15' × 20', and I've seen many recommendations for plots that measure 10' × 18' or or 10' × 15'. Remember, you can always squeeze in a few herbs in the flower beds if you're really cramped for space.

What do you want to grow in your garden? Which is too say, what do you want to eat? If nobody in your house will touch spinach, there's no point in planting it. Also, some vegetables like zucchini are very easy for beginners to grow; that is, they are prolific and require moderate or little care. Others are as temperamental as exotic hothouse blooms. Mercifully I haven't run across any of those, so I can't give you an example. And some simply might not be suitable for you or for your area. We wanted to grow asparagus until we found out that when it came in, you had to be there to pick the stalks every day. Since we were in the country only on weekends, we regretfully decided that asparagus was not the vegetable for us.

Now is the time to get out your seed catalogs. They contain a wealth of practical gardening information, and they do repay careful study. In them you can find old favorites that perhaps you remember from childhood, and you will discover the new varieties that the seedsmen bring out every year.

The professional horticulturalists and seed developers really deserve thanks from us for the improvements they have made. They have

PLANNING YOUR GARDEN

What are you going to plant?

Well, what do you like to eat?

bred resistance to disease and pests into many strains of vegetables, so that many problems that used to plague gardeners are now just a thing of the past. They have developed remarkable hybrids so that we can have sweet corn all summer, for instance. What I like are the seed tapes (originally developed for commercial growers), which are water soluble plastic tapes in which seeds are spaced at the correct planting intervals. These are terrific for small, hard to handle seeds like carrots and for budding gardeners like children. One of my favorite seed tapes is Park's Master Chef Lettuce blend, a tape that has four different kinds of lettuce seeds in it. In one quick trip down the garden row, I can pick four varieties of leaf lettuce for a truly mixed salad: dark green Bibb, apple green Simpson, frilled Salad Bowl, and wavy red Ruby.

Many companies also offer seed collections for special purposes and usually at reduced prices. Burpee's features a "Brag Patch Special for Children," which contains pumpkins, mammoth sunflowers, and zucchini. They also have a mini-vegetable garden for kids that will fit into a 5' × 6' area. Joseph Harris puts out a Pea Collection that features four varieties of peas that ripen in succession so that you can enjoy peas for a long while.

Now you can start planning on paper. Our list for our first year garden looked like this:

Beets
Carrots
Eggplant
Leaf Lettuce
Potatoes
Radishes
Peas
Onions
Sweet Peppers
Swiss Chard
Summer Squash
Pumpkin
Tomatoes

By July 4th, the radishes were gone and we had eaten our one cupful of peas, so I fertilized and replanted the rows. I put basil and marigolds where the radishes had been, and yellow wax beans where the peas were. By then the tomatoes had grown so that they shaded the eggplants and the peppers, so we moved them to the top quadrant of the garden where it was sunnier.

On August 15th, I actually wrote something in my gardening book, just as everybody, including myself, advises gardeners to do. The entry read: "Green bush beans are making second big crop. Yellow wax beans have blooms."

There are also these notes:

"Tomatoes planted next to squash do and don't need staking."

"One zucchini and two yellow squash stroyed by squash borers. I've bough vegetable-tomato dust to get rid of them."

Some people who live in a warmer clin than we do can actually put in a third gar but by the middle of August we are startin push toward the early frost dates. Also, by I am feeling rather "gardened out," as

WHERE TO GET

SEED

CATALOGS

Although you can buy seeds in your l stores, supermarkets, hardware stores, garden centers, you can also order t through the mail from the suppliers listed be Their catalogs describe in detail the var vegetable varieties, how they grow, mat dates, and all sorts of other helpful informa They also feature mouth-watering picture how your vegetables can—or should— when they grow up.

By comparing the offerings of var catalogs, you can, at your leisure, select exact type of vegetable you want—one th suited to your growing climate or your poses.

And, if nothing else, seed catalogs n great reading during those long winter mc when you can't do anything else.

Below is a list of the seed firms that I knc that have information available. Many of t offer catalogs free for the asking—so ask.

F.W. BOLGIANO & CO, 411 New York ⁄ N.E., Washington, D.C. This company, now of the Vaughan's Seed Company, feature America selections and planting information

BURGESS SEED AND PLANT CO., 20000, Galesburg, Miss., 49053 features sp pages on gourmet vegetables and novelty ieities.

W. ATLEE BURPEE CO., Philadelp 19132; Clinton, Iowa, 52732; or Riverside, Ca nia, 92502. Burpee maintains three office serve eastern, mid-western, and far wes customers respectively. It has one of the

as vegetables are concerned.

However, this does bring up an important point, and that is Succession Gardening. To take full advantage of your garden plot, you should keep it working—that is, growing things—at all times. When you have finished with one crop—say, radishes or peas, pull out the wasted plants, and add a good dose of soil nutrients or fertilizer to the planting row. Then plant a second crop—perhaps a vegetable that will come to maturity in the fall.

As you are planning your garden, separate the seed packets into piles marked "early, mid-season, or late," and mark your list accordingly. You can put the plants that take a long time to mature—pumpkin, for instance, or watermelon—off in a corner by themselves where they won't be disturbed. You can be more active in the rest of your garden. I put in an early crop, like peas, and then follow it with

---

most comprehensive catalogs ever, listing all the major and many of the minor varieties. They also sell many gardening supplies ranging from boots to cold frames. A basic book for your gardening library.

D.V. BURRELL SEED GROWERS, Box 150, Rocky Ford, Colorado, 81077 has a catalog that runs almost 100 pages. They give special emphasis to melons, tomatoes, and varieties suited to the west and southwest.

COMSTOCK, FERRE, AND CO., Wethersfield, Conn., 06109. Good bet for herbs; fair vegetable selection also.

DEGIORGI CO., INC., Council Bluffs, Iowa, 51501. A big catalog featuring prize winning seeds.

FARMER SEED AND NURSERY, Faribault, Minn., 55021. The company keeps in tune with the latest developments in experimental agricultural stations. The 80 page plus catalog gives special attention to early maturing vegetables and small compact types good for small-plot gardens.

HENRY FIELD SEED AND NURSERY, 407 Sycamore St., Shenandoah, Iowa, 51601. They put out a 100-plus-page catalog, with a wide variety selection, including many hard to find varieties. Also gives many gardening tips.

GURNEY SEED AND NURSERY COMPANY, 1448 Page St., Yankton, S.D., 57078. This catalog features many exotics and unusual vegetables, plus varieties suited to northern gardening seasons. Also features many gardening tips.

JOSEPH HARRIS COMPANY, INC., Moreton Farm, Rochester, N.Y. 14624. An excellent catalog, extremely informative and well designed. They emphasize varieties suitable for northeastern states.

J.J. JUNG SEED CO., Randolph, Wisc., 53956. A comprehensive catalog with information on newer introductions and localized variety choices.

KELLY BROTHERS NURSERIES, INC., Dansville, N.Y. 14437. Their catalog offers both seeds and nursery stock, plus good advice on growing vegetables.

EARL MAY SEED AND NURSERY COMPANY, 6032 Elm St., Shenandoah, Iowa, 51601

NICHOLS GARDEN NURSERY, 1190 North Pacific Highway, Albany, Oregon, 97321. They specialize in organic gardening, and their catalog features many unusual vegetable and herb seeds, including French, other European, and Oriental strains.

L.L. OLDS SEED CO., P.O. Box 1069, 2901 Packers Ave., Madison, Wisc., 53701. A large catalog, featuring many All America choices, plus good descriptive background on other varieties.

GEORGE W. PARK SEED CO., Greenwood, S.C., 29646. A long established Southern nursery that offers a wide selection of vegetable and flower seeds, plus a large range of indoor gardening items. They have interesting seed tapes and a section on miniature vegetables. Ask specifically for the vegetable catalog; they have serveral flower and plant catalogs as well.

ROSWELL SEED COL., P.O. Box 725, Roswell, N.M. 88201. The catalog emphasizes seeds suited to the Southwest.

SEEDWAY, INC., Hall, N.Y. 14463. This catalog has good planting instructions for vegetables featured.

R.H. SHUMWAY, Seedsman, 628 Cedar St., Rockford, Ill, 61101. This catalog is known as a gem for its quaint, old fashioned layout and illustrations. The format is big, thorough, and informative.

STARK BROTHERS NURSERIES AND ORCHARDS, Louisiana, Mo., 63353.

STOKES SEEDS, P.O. Box 548, Main Post Office, Buffalo, N.Y. 14240. This is a northern company with many Canadian customers, so you can expect to find short-season varieties here. Very comprhensive, including seeds untreated with fungicides.

OTIS TWILLEY SEED COMPANY, Salisbury, Md., 21801. Their catalog has useful information on varieties for disease resistance and varied growing conditions.

GLECKLERS SEEDMAN, Metamora, Ohio, 42540. They put out a small folder concentrating mainly on unique and unusual vegetables.

carrots. When a vegetable matures in mid-season, I try to replace it with a quick maturing crop like cress or radishes to take up the gardening and time slack.

Another method for successive plantings is to make successive sowings of the same vegetable for a continuous harvest. To make out your own planting guide, you'll need to know the frost dates in your area, and the maturity dates of the vegetables you wish to plant. (These will be in the seed catalogs and on the packet). And you'll need a calendar so you can count the days.

Below is a typical planting schedule that you can use as a guide to set up your own. Note that the first six vegetables—cabbage through spinach—are cool weather crops that should be planted four weeks before the last frost date in your area. The remaining four—tomatoes, squash, peppers and beans are tender plants that should be planted after all danger of frost is past.

PLANTING SCHEDULE

VARIETY (with days to maturity)	1st Planting	2nd Planting	3rd Planting
CABBAGE	April 15	July 15	(80 days)
LETTUCE (50 days)	April 15	June 15	Aug. 15
BEETS (60 days)	April 15	July 15	
CARROTS (75 days)	April 15	April 15	July 15
CHARD (60 days)	April 15		
RADISHES (25 days)	April 15	May 15	Aug. 15
ONIONS (14 days from planting to scallions, 80 days to onions)	April 15		
SPINACH (50 days)	April 15	Aug. 15	
TOMATOES (60 days)	May 15		
SQUASH (60 days)	May 15		
PEPPERS (60 days)	May 15		
BEANS (60 days)	May 15	July 15	

Dates are approximate and will vary according to location. Days to maturity will also vary according to varieties planted

Once you have decided *what* to put in your garden and *when* to put it in, you will have to decide *where* you want to put it.

As I mentioned earlier, the first step is to put your tall plants, like tomatoes or trellised cucumbers at the north end of the garden where they won't shade the smaller ones. Next, put your vine crops at the edges of the garden so they'll grow out rather than over valuable planting room.

The third step leads into an absolutely fascinating aspect of gardening that remains mysterious to scientists and gardeners alike. This is companion planting, which some gardeners view as a mixture of witchcraft and wishful thinking, and others view as simple hard fact. It is based on the observation that plants seem to have very strong likes and dislikes as far as other plants are concerned. Beans and carrots do well together, for instance, but beans do poorly near onions and garlic. Tomatoes, asparagus, and parsley are supposed to make a companionate threesome. Nastursiums and squash do well next to each other. We are all familiar with one of the earliest examples of companion planting: the practice of American Indians of putting squash, beans and corn together.

Why does this work—and does it? No one is sure, but some tentative explanations have been advanced. In the tomato-asparagus-parsley trio, it could be that the asparagus, with its deep root system, elnarges the feeding areas of the other plants with their shallower systems by plunging through compacting subsoil and loosening the ground. In the Indian's garden, the squash vines and heavy leaves acted as a living mulch to keep the roots of the corn and beans cool, which is the way they like it. Squash does well next to Nastursiums because the flowers' fragrance deters squash bugs.

Does it really work? I can't say for sure, but I did have a very curious experience with squash and nastursiums one summer.

We had put in a great deal of squash—acorn squash, bush patty pan, zucchini, and yellow crookneck. In a nearby corner of the garden I had planted a row of nastursiums, intending to transplant them into the squash patch. By the time the flower seedlings grew big enough, I was terrifically busy all over the garden, and and so only transplanted half the seedlings, and put them all on one side at that.

Everything flourished, until one fine day in August when I went out to the garden and discovered that the squash borer had invaded the garden. Those great tropical looking fronds were collapsing practically before my eyes.

This picture shows carrots actually being pulled from the row. Believe it or not, this picture was not staged, and was a random sample. The variety is King Imperator, and if this picture doesn't make your mouth water, I don't know what will.

Beets are a versatile vegetable. The roots are delicious, and we like the leaves cooked up as greens just as well.

Oswego is one of the most popular head lettuces for the home garden.

Frantically, I rushed back into the house to arm myself with vegetable dust to squirt at the pests, and knives and wires to dig them out of the stems of the plants. That was some way to spend a hot summer afternoon!

Although none of the plants actually died, the garden presented a distinctly lopsided appearance for the rest of the season. One half remained rather stunted and feeble, while the other half flourished madly. I was ready to take all the credit for rescuing my plants, when I noticed something unexpected.

The flourishing plants—those that had not been attacked by borers—were without exception next to the nastursiums I had transplanted earlier. The side of the garden that had suffered the most damage was the side where I had forgotten to put any of the flowers.

Is that conclusive proof of the value of companion planting? I don't think I could say that. I do think it is possible that the pests stayed away from the area where the fragrance—or stink, if you're a borer—of the nastursiums predominated.

Later I read that the protection against insects offered by companion planting is not 100% effective, but that's all right by me. If they do 90% or 80% or even 50% of the job of chasing away insects or helping each other to grow, I think that's just grand. The more they do, the less I have to worry. Besides, the nastursiums look pretty in a garden. (So do marigolds, which are real pest deterrents).

If you decide on companionate planting, it's good to get the friends right in there together. One way is to plant zig-zag rows, with the zigs and zags of the beets and onions tucked into one another. Another is to plant several companions in the same row. You might also decide to divide up your garden into loosely defined "sections." Put corn, squash, cucumbers, pumpkins, in one section (shades of the Indians!). In another, you could put strawberries, spinach, and beans. Put your paths in between these sections, rather than between companions. Ring your entire garden with a border of marigolds or other odiferous plants. Sprinkle these and other insect repelling herbs and flowers among the vegetables, checking the chart to make sure you're not near a foe instead of a friend.

The following will give you some ideas for making up your own companionate garden. Just remember that while your cucumbers like your peas, and your peas like your beans, and your beans like your potatoes, your potatoes just don't like cucumbers.

Marigolds are the workhorse of the garden, protecting it from all sorts of pests. Edge your vegetable plot with them, as shown here, faced down with white alyzzum.

Burpee Seeds

EARLY MATURING VEGETABLES

Early maturing vegetables are important in the far north where the growing season is short. In other sections they can be used to release space for later-sown crops, thus increasing garden productivity.

Vegetables which include varieties ready for harvest in two months or less after spring sowing are: Cress (20 days); Radish (22 days); Mustard Greens (35); Scallions (40); Loosehead Lettuce (40); Spinach (42); Turnips (35); Bush Snap Beans (48); Swiss Chard (50); Summer Squash (50); Cucumber (53); Early Peas (55); Beets (55); Kale (55); and Kohlrabi (55).

VEGETABLES FOR WINTER USE

While you are planning your seed order it's a good idea to include sufficient packets to make plantings that will provide vegetables you may store or leave in the garden during winter. Mulch root vegetables left in the garden to prevent alternate freezing and thawing. Dig them whenever you can get into the soil.

The following may be left in the garden and used during winter: Brussels Sprouts; Horse-Radish, Kale, Parsnips, Root Parsley, and Salsify.

Vegetables that store well for winter use include: Winter Cabbage; Carrots; Celery; Chicory Sugarhat; Onions and Shallots; Parsnips; Pumpkins; Radishes, White Chinese and Round Black Spanish; Rutabaga; Winter Squash; and Turnips.

A GENEROUS GARDEN FOR A FAMILY OF FOUR

One of the regular contributors to the magazine "Organic Gardening and Farming" gave the following as her planting list. This is what we all can aspire to, although, as she noted, "You may find that you can plant less for four people. I tend to overplant. The amounts listed take care of my family of four and plenty of guests, with some surplus to give away and sell." Her garden, incidentally, covers ¼ acre.

Beets .... 180 ft.
Broccoli .... 40 to 50 plants
Carrots .... 200-300 ft.
Cauliflower .... 20-40 plants
Celery .... 30 plants
Cherry pepper .... 20 ft.
Cucumbers .... 30 hills
Dill .... 20 ft.
Early cabbage .... 60 ft.
Eat-all pumpkins for seed .... 10-20 hills
Eggplant .... 12-15 plants
Endive .... 15 ft.
Garlic .... 40 ft., double row
Head lettuce .... 60 ft.
Hot pepper .... 20 ft.
Kale .... 15-20 ft.
Kohlrabi .... 20-35 ft.
Leaf lettuce .... 120-150 ft.
Lima beans .... 60 ft.
Muskmelon .... 20-40 hills
Parsley .... 30 ft.
Parsnips .... 40 ft.
Potatoes .... 40-90 lb. seed potatoes
Radishes .... 100 ft.
Regular peas .... 150 ft.
Rutabagas .... 20 ft.
Salsify .... 20-30 ft.
Scallions .... 2 lb. sets
Snap beans .... 160-250 ft.
Soybeans .... 200 ft.
Sugar peas .... 150 ft.
Summer squash .... 70 ft. row
Sweet corn .... 2-3,000 ft. of row
Sweet onions .... 4 bunches
Sweet pepper .... 40 ft.
Tomatoes ... 140 ft. row (We give away a lot!)
Turnips .... 60 ft.
Winter squash .... 15-20 hills ●

EASY TO GROW VEGETABLES

Bush Beans	Kale
Beets	Leaf Lettuce
Carrots	Pumpkin
Collards	Radish
Corn	Rutabaga
Cucumber	Squash
Curlycress	Swiss Chard
Dill	Turnip

Northrup, King, Inc.

GOOD FOR WINTER STORAGE IN A COOL FROST FREE PLACE

Beets	Pumpkins
Cabbage	Rutabaga
Carrots	Winter Radish
Celery	Winter Squash
Onions	Turnips
Parsnips	

GREATEST YIELDS FOR SPACE AND EFFORT

Bush Snap Beans	Onions Sets
Beets	Swiss Chard
Carrots	Tomatoes
Cucumber (Supported)	Zucchini Squash
Lettuce	

Look how these beets have grown. That's why you need to thin them to stand two to three inches apart in the row.

A COMPANIONATE HERBAL FOR THE ORGANIC GARDEN

A list of herbs, their companions, their uses, including some beneficial weeds and flowers.

BASIL: Companion to tomatoes; dislikes rue intensely. Improves growth and flavor. Repels flies and mosquitoes.

BEEBALM: Companion to tomatoes; improves growth and flavor.

BORAGE: Companion to tomatoes, squash and strawberries; deters tomato worm; improves growth and flavor.

CARAWAY: Plant here and there; loosens soil.

CATNIP: Plant in borders; deters flea beetle.

CAMOMILE: Companion to cabbages and onions; improves growth and flavor.

CHERVIL: Companion to radishes; improves growth and flavor.

CHIVES: Companion to carrots; improves growth and flavor.

DEAD NETTLE: Companion to potatoes; deters potato bug; improves growth and flavor.

DILL: Companion to cabbage; dislikes carrots; improves growth and health of cabbage.

FENNEL: Plant away from gardens. Most plants dislike it.

FLAX: Companion to carrots, potatoes; deters potato bug. Improves growth and flavor.

GARLIC: Plant near roses and raspberries; deters Japanese beetle; improves growth and health.

HORSERADISH: Plant at corners of potato patch to deter potato bug.

HENBIT: General insect repellant.

HYSSOP: Deters cabbage moth; companion to cabbage and grapes. Keep away from radishes.

LAMB'S-QUARTERS: This edible weed

A List of Common Garden Vegetables, Their Companions and Their Antagonists

VEGETABLE	LIKES	DISLIKES
Asparagus	Tomatoes, Parsley, basil	
Beans	Potatoes, carrots, cucumbers, cauliflower, cabbage, summer savory, most other vegetables and herbs	Onion, garlic, gladiolus
Pole Beans	Corn, summer savory	Onions, beets, kohlrabi, sunflower
Bush Beans	Potatoes, cucumbers, corn, strawberries, celery, summer savory	Onions
Beets	Onions, Kohlrabi	Pole beans
Cabbage Family (Cabbage, cauliflower, kale, kohlrabi, broccoli, Brussels sprouts)	Aromatic plants, potatoes, celery dill, camomile, sage, peppermint, rosemary, beets, onions	Strawberries, tomatoes, pole beans
Carrots	Peas, leaf lettuce, chives, onions, leek, rosemary, sage, tomatoes	Dill
Celery	Leek, tomatoes, bush beans, cauliflower, cabbage	
Chives	Carrots	Peas, beans
Corn	Potatoes, peas, beans, cucumbers, pumpkin, squash	
Cucumbers	Beans, corn, peas, radishes, sunflowers	Potatoes, aromatic herbs
Tomato	Chives, onion, parsley, asparagus, marigold, nasturtium, carrot	Kohlrabi, potato, fennel, cabbage
Eggplant	Beans	
Peas	Carrots, turnips, radishes, cucumbers, corn, beans, most vegetables and herbs	Onions, garlic, gladiolus, potato

Plant	Companions	Incompatible
Squash	Nasturtium, corn	
Onion (including garlic)	Beets, strawberries, tomato, lettuce, summer savory, camomile (sparsely)	Peas, beans
Leek	Onions, celery, carrots	
Lettuce	Carrots and radishes (lettuce, carrots and radishes make a strong team grown together); strawberries, cucumbers	
Radish	Peas, nasturtium, lettuce, cucumbers	
Parsley	Tomato, asparagus	
Potato	Beans, corn, cabbage, horseradish (should be planted at corners of patch), marigold, eggplant (as a lure for Colorado potato beetle)	Pumpkin, squash, cucumber, sunflower, tomato, raspberry
Pumpkin	Corn	Potato
Soybeans	Grows with anything, helps everything	
Strawberries	Bush bean, spinach, borage, lettuce (as a border)	
Spinach	Strawberries	
Sunflower	Cucumbers	Potato
Turnip	Peas	

should be allowed to grow in moderate amounts in the garden, especially in corn.

LEMON BALM: Sprinkle throughout garden.

LOVAGE: Improves flavor and health of plants if planted here and there.

MARIGOLDS: The workhorse of the pest deterrents. Plant throughout garden, it discourages Mexican bean beetles, nematodes and other insects.

MINT: Companion to cabbage and tomatoes; improves health and flavor; deters white cabbage moth.

MARJORAM: Here and there in garden; improves flavors.

MOLE PLANT: Deters moles and mice if planted here and there.

NASTURTIUM: Companion to radishes, cabbage and curcurbits; plant under fruit trees. Deters aphids, squash bugs, striped pumpkin beetles. Improves growth and flavor.

PETUNIA: Protects beans.

POT MARIGOLD: Companion to tomatoes, but plant elsewhere in garden, too. Deters asparagus beetle, tomato worm and general garden pests.

PURSLANE: This edible weed makes good ground cover in the corn.

PIGWEED: One of the best weeds for pumping nutrients from the subsoil, it is especially beneficial to potatoes, onions and corn. Keep weeds thinned.

PEPPERMINT: Planted among cabbages, it repels the white cabbage butterfly.

ROSEMARY: Companion to cabbage, bean, carrots and sage; deters cabbage moth, bean beetles and carrot fly.

RUE: Keep it far away from Sweet Basil; plant near roses and raspberries; deters Japanese beetle.

SAGE: Plant with rosemary, cabbage and carrots; keep away from cucumbers. Deters cabbage moth, carrot fly.

SOUTHERNWOOD: Plant here and there in garden; companion to cabbage; improves growth and flavor; deters cabbage moth.

SOWTHISTLE: This weed in moderate amounts can help tomatoes, onions and corn.

SUMMER SAVORY: Plant with beans and onions; improves growth and flavor. Deters bean beetles.

TANSY: Plant under fruit trees; companion to roses and raspberries. Deters flying insects, Japanese beetles, striped cucumber beetles, squash bugs, ants.

TARRAGON: Good throughout garden.

THYME: Here and there in garden. It deters cabbage worm.

VALERIAN: Good anywhere in garden.

WILD MORNING GLORY: Allow it to grow in corn.

WORMWOOD: As a border, it keeps animals from the garden.

YARROW: Plant along borders, paths, near aromatic herbs; enhances essential oil production.

Chapter Five

PREPARING

YOUR

GARDEN

. . . or,

doing the spadework

There are basically two ways of preparing your garden: by hand, or with a machine, such as a rototiller. We've done it both ways, and each method has something to be said for it.

For small areas, you'll probably do just as well with a spade and a pitchfork (the latter is particularly good if you have rocky soil), plus a rake to smooth the topsoil for a a fine seedbed. These are basic tools that are easy to operate and don't cost much. If you're a beginner, don't invest in a lot of expensive, heavy duty equipment that can run into hundreds of dollars. You can always graduate to that level later.

In addition to what I've suggested, the USDA recommends getting a "7 inch common hoe, a strong cord for laying off rows, a wheelbarrow, and a garden hose long enough to water all parts of the garden." We have those, with the exception of the hoe, which we don't need because we mulch. A trowel for transplanting seedlings is also handy.'

Since you don't need very much, it makes sense to get the very best tools that you can find. This is no place to save pennies. Good tools, well designed and of high grade manufacture and materials, will make the work that you will have to do in the garden easier and more efficient. Good tools also last a lot longer than cheap ones.

Like most people, I had to learn this the hard way. I kept buying inexpensive garden clippers at about $2 a pair because I just couldn't bear to part with the $10 for a really good pair. When I realized that I was developing an expensive collection of broken and disabled clippers that could barely snip a zinnia from its bush, I finally invested in the good pair.

If you've never dug up a garden, here's how: Mark off the boundaries by driving a stake or stick into each corner, and run a string from one post to another. Now start at one end with your spade and turn the soil over to a depth of one foot. Shake the soil off the sod (if any), throw that away, throw away the rocks, and repeat. And repeat. And repeat. Once that's all done, you add the soil conditioners and nutrients as described in the previous chapter, and turn those into the soil, too. Now rake the top smooth and you're ready to plant.

It sounds easy, but digging a garden by hand takes time. Bill volunteered to dig up our first garden, figuring that it would only take him a weekend. Three weekends later, he finally got to the end.

Part of his problem was that the site we selected for our garden (sunny, convenient to the house) was rich in New England's most

This is Nancy Thurber, canning and preserving expert of the Garden Way Manufacturing Co., with a Troy-Bilt Roto Tiller. Unlike other tillers, the Troy-Bilt is sold almost entirely through the mail, direct from the factory, Garden Way Mfg. Co., 102nd St. and Ninth Ave., Troy, N.Y. 12180.

notable resource: rocks. Those picturesque stone walls that one sees all over our part of northern Connecticut and elsewhere in New England were once the bane of many a farmer's life.

When Bill was through, there was simply no question of taking them away—he must have gotten half a ton of rocks out of that garden. We couldn't just let them stay there in an ugly pile, so we tried to use them. I edged the flower beds and part of the driveway with rocks about the size of a sneaker. Flat rocks, as big as dinner plates, made a path that runs along the west side of the house. A few of the mammoth ones went to repair the stone wall (yes, we have one, too) that runs across the front yard. I dug dry wells under each and every gutter downspout and filled *them* with rocks. And believe it or not, we still have a pile of potato-sized rocks that continue to baffle me. I would welcome any suggestions on the creative use of rocks.

In any case, the following year we made a second garden. This time Bill hired a local farmer to do the job with his rototiller. You can rent rototillers and do the job yourself, but it seemed to us that hiring someone with his very own equipment made more sense. The costs were not much higher, and we didn't have to fetch it, operate it, or take the thing back. (They are very heavy, if you're not familiar with one). My friend in Philadelphia rototilled her own garden last year; she reported that the next day she felt as though she had been beaten all over with rubber hoses. (If you want to rent, try equipment rental agencies, hardware stores, or local garden center. Check the yellow Pages under Rental Service Stores and Yards.)

When should you start your garden? We began our first one in the spring, just before we wanted to plant. I think that's one reason why digging it up became such a job. There was so much pressure to get it done right away. While Bill was out there digging, I was waiting impatiently for him to finish so that I could start planting.

Incidentally, you should not work your soil while it is wet—unless the work will certainly be followed by a severe freeze. To tell if it's ready in the spring, the usual test is to squeeze together a handful of soil. If it sticks together in a ball and does not readily crumble under slight pressure by the thumb and finger, it is too wet to be worked. If you're in any doubt, dig down a little bit and test the soil under the surface. The surface may be dry enough, but the lower layers may be too wet for working.

If you disturb the soil while it's too wet, you will wind up with great, sticky clods of earth. In due time these will dry out—into great, rocklike clods of earth. So be patient in the spring.

The second garden we had rototilled in October, when the work would be followed by a severe freeze. And we left it open to let the natural elements—rain, snow, sun, wind—"mellow the soil." I didn't understand why this would happen, until I read recently that snow is often called the "poor man's manure." Why? Well, according to Joan Lee Faust, the gardening editor of the New York Times:

"Snow is a good thermal insulator, a sort of nature's blanket. It forms as frozen water vapor and reaches the ground as hexagonally shaped ice crystals. Several crystals join to make a snowflake.

"Snow melts with a slow trickle and penetrates deeply into the subsoil without danger of erosion that comes from heavy rain, although it takes much more snow, about 30 inches, to equal one inch of rainfall. In addition, the freezing and thawing action of snow acts on the physical texture of plowed soil. For all these reasons, snow is often called the "poor man's manure."

One more kind to add to our list!

If you can get a season's jump on starting your garden, you'll find your task a lot easier. For instance, the easiest way to turn lawn or sod into a planting bed is to cover the area with leaves, straw, heavy plastic, old linoleum, carpet remnants, or newspapers—just about any thing you have around that will make an opaque mulch. The mulch will not only smother the grasses, it will also start to rot them down for you. In the spring all you may have to do is to work this decayed material into the ground along with compost and fertilizers. Before you know it, you'll be ready to plant!

One of my neighbors put down a few layers of newspapers in the fall and covered them over with some old blankets so they wouldn't blow away. In the spring he pulled off the blankets and papers, and started a queen-sized herb patch right outside his kitchen.

The most amazing story I ever heard concerns a gardener who raked all his leaves into a foot-thick pile over a sod area one fall. The following June, he decided his garden was ready, but didn't even bother to spade up the area. All he did was to dig a hole for each tomato bush, pop it in, and pull the leaves back around as a mulch. He was rewarded with an excellent crop. By the time frost hit in the fall, the leaf-mulch—and the underlying sod—had completely decomposed into the soil. If you have ever tried to dig up sod, you will appreciate what an achievement this was. Sod has roots that seem like sheets of Brillo when you are trying to dig them out—so tenacious, strong, and resistant as are they.

Anyway, he then pulled the old tomato vines into a heap, ground them up with his rotary mower, and then rototilled the ground as easily as though it had been plowed earlier. The next spring he rototilled a fine seed bed with just one pass of the machine, which I understand is quite unusual.

That is truly the lazy man's—or the clever gardener's—way to put in a garden.

But suppose it's a clear, sunny day in May, and you've got a yen to do a little digging—not a huge amount, but just a little. Well, you can do just that. You can dig up and thoroughly prepare a small 4' × 4' "postage stamp" garden that will hold all your herbs, or a crop of carrots. If that's too much work, you can dig out a generous hole, condition the soil there, and put in a tomato plant or a couple of zucchini seeds. It may not seem like a lot, but wait until you start picking the harvest. You'll get much more than you expected from your little bit of digging! ●

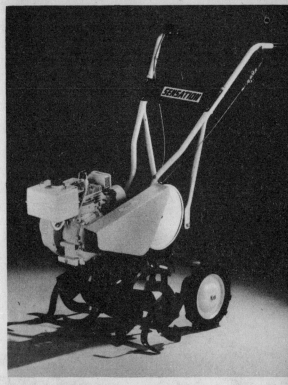

This is an example of a front-end rototiller. They are used to break up sod, turn over gardens in the spring, and work autumn leaves into garden soil in the fall.

Each 3 × 10 inch plastic tray holds 12
"Bio-Gros." This smaller size, economical seed
starter is space saving and suitable for
growing annuals and houseplant seedlings.
The finest horticultural invention for starting
seeds since "One-Steps," "Bio-Gros" are
completely biodegradable. Longer peat fibers
eliminate the need for the plastic net.

Park Seeds

Today, there are all sorts of fancy scientific aids that will tell you when it's time to plant. There are frost date maps, and hardiness maps, charts and tables, and many more. Some of those I've included here. There are also some old reliable signs that Mother Nature puts up for us to follow—if we know how to read them. I've included some of the ones I've heard of; you might ask any old timey gardeners in your area for the natural signs *they* follow.

It's important to time your plantings because vegetables fall into two groups—cool weather crops and hot weather crops. The cool weather lovers are hardy vegetables that actually thrive and do well when the weather is chilly. These include most of the root and leafy vegetables, such as beets, carrots, and spinach. The hot weather lovers are the tender ones, that need lots of sun and warm weather to blossom and form fruits. These include beans, tomatoes, and squash.

(The one exception seems to be peas, which enjoy cool weather but produce blossoms and fruits. The explanation is that when the weather is cool and the days short, these plants put all their efforts into making roots and leaves. When the days start to warm up, they smile, blossom, and go to seed. That is, peas).

To figure out the planting dates in your area, you'll need a frost free map and a chart

WHEN AND HOW TO PLANT

e Seeds

It's fun to start seeds indoors. You can order an entire "outfit" like the one shown above, or you can improvise with egg cartons old popsicle sticks, and a home-mixed growing medium.

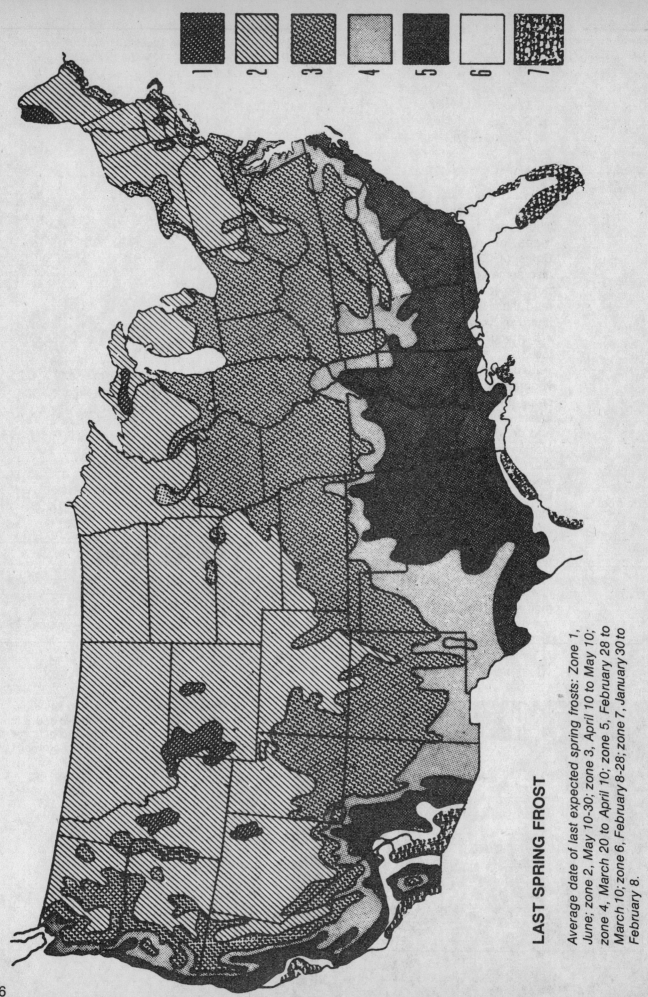

LAST SPRING FROST

Average date of last expected spring frosts: Zone 1, June; zone 2, May 10-30; zone 3, April 10 to May 10; zone 4, March 20 to April 10; zone 5, February 28 to March 10; zone 6, February 8-28; zone 7, January 30 to February 8.

showing the approximate planting dates for most vegetables. Find out where you are on the map and determine the average date of the last killing frost. For instance, we live in zone 2, which means that our last frost date falls between May 15 and May 31. Experience has shown that we are safer choosing May 31 as the last frost date. By referring to the chart, I find that the very earliest I can put in peas is April 15. (However, great numbers of the pea-raising public holds out for planting on St. Patrick's Day—March 17.)

Keep in mind that the map is only a rough guide. Climactic conditions can vary wildly within one zone, depending on your elevation, proximity to water and other factors. For that matter, conditions can vary wildly on the same piece of property. Our land slopes upward from the road, from north to south. Down by the road where the ground is also shaded by 40-foot hemlocks there is a frost pocket where snow stays on the ground until late spring. At the top of the hill, the sun shines brightly all day long on a table-flat meadow, and makes a sun pocket.

If you are planning to make additional plantings during the summer, you'll also have to know the early frost date in your area.

If you plant too close to that date, your plants possibly won't mature or will be killed by the frost.

Accurate counting does help, I can tell you, because I made a very foolish error two summers in a row because I didn't. Many books, articles and seed catalogs recommended planting kale as a second crop in the summer for fall use, as in "peas followed by kale." I didn't bother to count the days until the first frost, but just planted kale in July after the peas came out. The plants came up, flourished, and then simply stopped growing when the frost hit in mid-September. They weren't killed, they just stopped. I remembered that the garden books all said that "flavor improved after frost," so I remained quite pleased with my little babies.

At least I was until I stopped by the local vegetable stand run by three generations of farmers. The farmer strode in holding a single plant of kale in each hand. I gasped. Each plant measured 2½ feet across, and was made up of enormous, ruffled fronds. They were simply beautiful; like green bridal bouquets for a giant.

When I got home, I consulted all my charts and maps. I was really in shock and despair. Where had I gone wrong? I finally realized that in my zone, kale could be planted as a fall crop no later than June 15. After the peas, meaning mid-July for me, was about a month too late. So watch your frost dates at both ends!

Incidentally, as you are making up your seed order, remember that in addition to warm sea-

APPROXIMATE PLANTING TIMES OF POPULAR VEGETABLES					
Cold-hardy plants for early-spring planting		Cold-tender or heat-hardy plants for late-spring or early-summer planting			Hardy plants for late-summer or fall planting except in the North (plant 6 to 8 weeks before first fall freeze)
Very hardy (plant 4 to 6 weeks before frost-free date)	Hardy (plant 2 to 4 weeks before frost-free date)	Not cold-hardy (plant on frost-free date)	Requir-ing hot weather (plant 1 week or more after frost-free date)	Medium heat tolerant (good for summer planting)	
Broccoli Cabbage Lettuce Onions Peas Potatoes Spinach Turnips	Beets Carrots Chard Mustard Parsnips Radishes Peas Leaf Lettuce	Beans, snap Cucum-bers Okra New Zea-land spinach Soybeans Squash Sweet corn Tomatoes	Beans, lima Eggplant Peppers Sweetpo-tatoes	Beans, all Chard Soybeans New Zea-land spinach Squash Sweet corn	Beets Collards Kale Lettuce Mustard Spinach Turnips

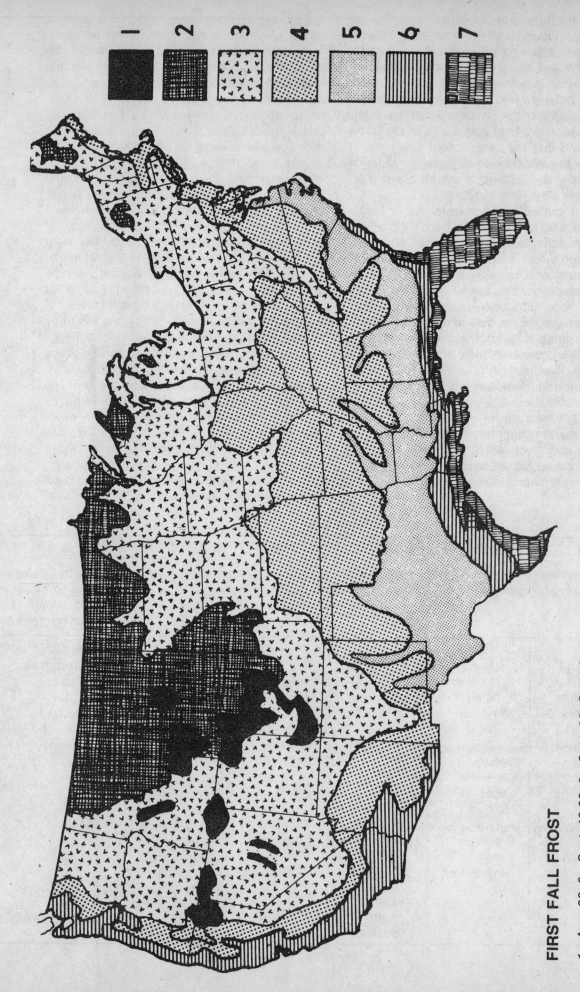

FIRST FALL FROST

1—Aug. 30; 2—Sept. 10-20; 3—Sept. 30, Oct. 10;
4—Oct. 20-30; 5—Oct. 30, Nov. 10; 6—Nov. 20, Dec.
10; 7—Dec. 10-20. Dates given here are subject to
local conditions and weather cycles.

son and cool season vegetables, we also have early and late varieties of many of them. The early varieties require less heat to mature than do the late. If you want to start your garden early, you can begin with one of the early varieties, then follow through with a later-maturing variety for a season-long harvest of the same crop. (Or you can put in a quide succession crop.)

If you are interested in more detailed instructions along this line, the USDA puts out an excellent booklet containing detailed lists of planting dates for various vegetables for the entire country. The booklet is the Home and Garden Bulletin No. 202, "Growing Vegetables in the Home Garden." You can get it by writing the Superintendent of Documents, U.S. Government Printing Office, Washington, D.C. 20402. The price is 80¢. The government puts out a great deal of free and/or inexpensive practical information on gardening.

For those who prefer to rely on Mother Nature's signals, here we go. This guide relies on the blooming or spring development of fairly common trees and plants, and certainly predates the USDA and all our scientists.

There is a lovely tree, called the Shadbush, that covers itself with white blossoms in the spring. The Indians named it the Shadbush tree, because when it bloomed, they knew the shad fish were running in the Hudson River. At least that's the story.

And now for the story on vegetables:

WHAT TO LOOK FOR:
Development of color in flowers from spring bulbs like tulips and narcissus
Appearance of plum and cherry blossoms
Oak leaves come out
Appearance of apple, cherry, quince, and strawberry blossoms

WHAT TO PLANT:
Plant beets, carrots, leaf lettuce, onions, peas, radishes and spinach
Plant head lettuce
Plant snap beans, okra, New Zealand spinach, tomatoes
Plant everything else—cucumbers, melons, eggplant, and peppers.

As you can see, you'll have plenty of time over the season to plant your garden. In fact, by the time you get the last plants and seeds in, you may well be harvesting the first ones you planted. And that's a terrific feeling!

The actual business of planting, however, inspires mixed feelings—in me, at least. Trans-

Harris Seeds

Starting seedlings indoors can be lots of fun, if you have a sunny window or a flourescent light set-up. Here is a typical seed-starting kit from Harris Seeds that includes everything you need to grow 72 sturdy seedlings. Note the greenhouse made from a plastic bag at left to keep moisture and temperature more even.

Jiffy Products of America

These are Jiffy-7 pellets, a popular way of starting seeds indoors, shown prepacked in trays of ten. Add a little water to the pellets, wait a few minutes for them to soak up, and your miniature pots are ready for seeds or seedlings. The bottoms are slotted for drainage.

planting flats of flowers and vegetables in late May and early June is very rewarding, satisfying work. The weather is usually sunny and mild, so that being out of doors is a pleasure. In addition, you can see the results of your labors immediately: rows of orange marigolds and patches of feathery tomato seedlings. But late spring, when the hardy vegetables and seeds go in, is another story. I still remember one day in late April, with brisk winds whipping everything about. I was on my hands and knees in the garden, poking onion sets into the damp, cold ground. My hands were blue with cold, my back was beginning to hurt from bending over so, and when I leaned back to admire my labors, there was nothing to be seen. The onions, naturally enough, were all underground where I had put them.

Nevertheless, we must sow if we are to reap, so here is how you go about it.

Some seeds you must plant directly into the ground, as they don't take well to transplanting. These include the root crops, like beets, carrots, and radishes; and those with really big seeds, such as beans, peas, and corn.

Let's assume that you've got your garden all prepared.

The night before you are ready to plant, soak your seeds overnight in water. They will germinate much faster.

The next day, check the seed package to see how far apart you should space your rows. Get some old sticks or stakes, and pound them in at the proper intervals along each side of your garden. Now stretch a string between the opposite stakes, which will show you exactly where to plant your rows. They will be nice and straight.

With the place staked out (you can do this row by row, incidentally), consult your seed packet again to see how deeply and how to space the seeds. Make a furrow of the proper

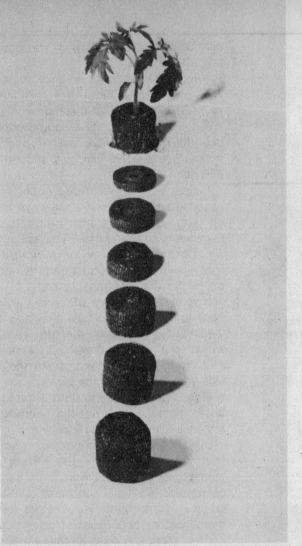

You will have fun raising your own plants with ark Seed Starter Kits. Just add water to each ellet and stand back. They'll expand to seven times their height in minutes. Drop a few seeds on each and give light and moisture until plants are ready for the garden or larger houseplant containers. Roots grow right through the growing medium into the soil. Each tray holds plants in a slightly elevated position so that they soak up the right amount of moisture from the bottom of the tray, thus insuring quick seed germination and plant growth. An electric heating cable spread beneath the trays provides gentle warmth on indow sills or under Gro-Lamps. The best yet grow consistently healthy plants from seeds.

This husky tomato seedling is ready to be set out into the garden, peat pot and all. Note how the roots grow right through the sides of the pot.

depth, using the end of your rake handle or a stick, and drop the seeds in. Learning to sprinkle the fine seeds in evenly—like carrots—takes practice, but you will learn eventually. If they're in too thick, you'll just thin them out later on. (This is where seed tapes are useful).

We found that a handy way of spacing the big seeds, like peas and beans—is to break off a twig for the desired length—say 3" for beans—as use it as a measuring rod. Even small children can space seeds correctly with this gadget.

Now cover the seeds with the soil along the side of the furrow, and tamp down the earth, either by walking along the row or by pressing the seeds down lightly with a piece of board. Water gently, and pull your hay mulch up alongside of the planting rows.

That's it. Don't forget to label the rows so you'll know what's planted where. You'd be surprised how quickly you can forget. If we've used up all the seeds in the packet, we simply pop the paper envelope over one of the sticks, or else we make a sign.

Some vegetables, such as broccoli, brussels sprouts, cabbage, cauliflower, eggplant, peppers, and tomatoes, seem to get off to a better start if they are first grown from seeds indoors and then transplanted into the garden as seedlings. In areas where the growing season is short, such as ours, we absolutely must put these in as seedlings if we are going to get any kind of harvest at all.

Fortunately, you can buy flats of seedlings of the most popular varieties of vegetables (and flowers) at garden centers and nurseries. To transplant them, make a hole big enough to accomodate the roots freely, using a pointed stick, your hands, or a trowel. To give the seedlings an extra boost at this time, you can put a trowelful of compost in the bottom of the planting hole, or you can can give them a dose of a mild liquid fertilizer. (Careful, you don't want to burn the roots).

Here's one recipe for an easy starter solution: Add one pound of 5-10-5 fertilizer to one gallon of water and let it stand overnight to dissolve. The next day stir it up and pour the concentrate into four more gallons of water. This makes five gallons, which is enough for about 150 plants.

Incidentally, when transplanting a plant or seedling of any size at all, always fill the hole up with water or starter solution and let it completely soak in before you set in the plant. This provides plenty of moisture for the roots—where the plant needs it—and so reduces the shock of transplanting.

If your seedlings are really tiny, you may not have to dig much of a hole. You may do just as well poking a hole in the dirt with a dibble, which is a stick or dowel with a point on the end. With your left hand, make the hole, and with your right, pop in the plant.

One final word: Try to disturb the roots as little as possible, and set the seedling in at its previous level or even a little below.

But suppose that you want to try some plants that you can't find in the nurseries come spring? For instance, I want to try some midget cucumbers, so that I can make cornichons this summer. Cornichons, if you're not familiar with them, are tiny sour French pickles that cost the earth in specialty food stores, although I can't imagine why. But they do, so that means I must start the seeds indoors myself.

Here's how. First of all, determine the average date of the last frost in your area. That's the key to starting your seeds indoors. Check the seed packet for the number of days required for germination. (Don't assume anything; the time for germination of different vegetables varies considerably). To this number add 18 more days to allow for the seedling to develop to transplantable size. The total is the number of days before the average last frost date to start seed indoors.

If, when the last frost date rolls around, you have a few more seedlings than will be needed, you can plant the extra ones in the garden then. But if you don't have any extras with which to gamble, wait a few days after the average frost date to set out what you have. If the weather remains mild, you will have an earlier crop and a bigger crop then you had gambled on. If frost strikes them down, you will still have some reserves inside.

If you have any doubts at all about the weather, you should protect your seedlings by setting bottomless plastic milk jugs over them.

Starting seeds indoors is basically simple—*if* you have ample light. If you do not have a sunny, south-facing window or flourescent lights, then you are in trouble.

For your seedbed you can use any wide, shallow container you have—metal foil pans, shallow flower pots, or wooden flats. They must have drainage holes on the bottom, so make them now, if necessary. Put a layer of gravel or broken clay flower pots in the bottom, and fill up to the top with potting soil or some of the special soil mixes you will see in the garden centers. Water well, and let the water drain out.

Sprinkle seeds lightly over the surface and cover them with a thick layer of the potting soil no deeper than three times the thickness of the seed. Keep the surface moist at all times. If the germinating seeds or the developing plants dry out, they will die. To keep moisture in before the plants sprout, you can cover the container with a sheet of newspaper or plastic wrap to retain moisture. When the seedlings emerge, take off the newspaper, although you can leave the clear plastic wrap on for a few days if you want. Now put the container in your sunniest window, or three to four inches under flourescent lights.

When the second pair of leaves appears, you can transplant the seedlings to individual peat pots or into a another flat, spacing them two inches apart.

If this seems like a lot of work (and it is, for the beginner), there are easier ways. One is the starter kits, available in many stores and through some catalogs, that have container, soil, and seeds altogether. Some have been preplanted, so that all you have to do is take the top off and water the soil. Some have the seeds in a separate packet that you sow yourself, so make sure you know which kind you've got before you start watering.

You can also start your seeds in individual peat pots and some of these, like jiffy pellets, come with a growing medium inside. Then all you do is drop two or three seeds in each pot, water, thin, and watch them grow. When you are ready to transplant into the garden, you set out the whole works, pot included. The roots will grow through the sides of the pot, and you will greatly minimize the shock of transplanting.

Garden stores and seed catalogs carry impressive arrays of all sorts of items that make the job of starting seeds indoors much easier. While I really find them irrestible, I have tried to spare my wallet and improve my mind by devising substitutes that don't cost anything. Sometimes I succeed, and sometimes I succumb to temptation, under the guise of Inquiring Scientist making Useful Experiments. For the the ideas that succeeded, see the chapter on Dirt Cheap Gardening Ideas. ●

It took us only a season—or maybe it was about a week or two—of working in a garden to realize that we needed all the help we could get. If you don't utilize every scrap of aid possible, there is no end to the amount of time, effort, and hard physical labor you can spend in a garden.

We simply didn't have the time, since we were there only on weekends. We certainly couldn't hire someone to come in and garden for us (nor did we want to), and we reregarded the chemical controls (poisons) with some trepidation. We were afraid to risk poisoning ourselves, the cat, the children, the birds, the racoon, the 'possum, and so on by indiscriminate spraying. But what to do?

Somewhere around this point I realized that the hoary old phrase "working with nature" (which always sounded too high-minded and preachy for me) could easily be reworded to read "Let nature work for you." Letting nature do the work that otherwise would fall to me made wonderful sense. Mulching with hay was a good example of letting natural processes take over the jobs of keeping the soil moist, friable, fertile, and aerated.

As I played with this idea, I began to realize how much work nature would do for me if I encouraged her even just a little bit.

Companion planting was one way. If putting peas and carrots together helped them both grow better, then in they'd go together. If certain plants would repel various insects, they would go in also. I was absolutely fascinated when I found that marigolds repelled a parasite called nematodes by exuding a certain

Chapter Seven

LETTING NATURE
WORK FOR YOU

WHERE TO GET PREDATOR INSECTS AND WORMS

LACEWING FLIES

California Green Lacewings, Inc., 2521 Webb Ave., Alameda, California, 95401

Fairfax Biological Laboratory, Clinton Corners, New York, 12514

Gothard, Inc., P.O. Box 370, Canutillo, Texas 79835

LADYBUGS

Bio-Control Company, Rte. 2, Box 2397, Auburn, California, 95603

W. Atlee Burpee Company (addresses above)

Gurney Seed & Nursery (address above)

Paul Harris, P.O. Box 1495, Marysville, California 95901

Lakeland Nurseries Sales, Hanover, Pa., 17331

PRAYING MANTISES

Bio-Control Company (address above)

W. Atlee Burpee Company (addresses above)

Eastern Biological Control Company, Route 5, Box 379, Jackson, N.J. 08527

Gurney Seed & Nursery (address above)

Gothard, Inc. (address above)

TRICHOGAMMA WASPS

Fairfax Biological Laboratory (address above)

Gothard, Inc. (address above)

WORMS

Gurney's Seed & Nursery Co. (address above)

Lakeland Nurseries Sales, (address above)

Stern's Nurseries, Geneva, New York, 14456

---

substance from their roots (this has been scientifically documented, by the way). We have faithfully planted marigolds amongst the vegetables, and, to paraphrase the old jingle about a Purple Cow,

I never saw a nematode
I never hope to see one;
But I can tell you anyhow,
I'd rather see than be one.

Did you know that white geraniums—not pink or red but white geraniums—will deter Japanese Beetles? I didn't know that either until I read Thalassa Cruso's book "Making Things Grow Outdoors." I have not tried it, but I will, and I pass it on for what it is worth.

One of the best ways to foil various pests and plant diseases is to plant seeds that are resistant to those problems. The information should appear on the seed packet itself if you're buying seeds at the local hardware store. The seed catalogs are an absolute goldmine of information on disease resistant strains. If you know that a particular plant ailment is common in your area, you may be able to find a variety that carries resistance to that ailment.

Another great ally in the gardener's fight against destructive insects are the birds. We started feeding the birds by accident. In the course of Bill's labors on Wall Street, he had inadvertently acquired a bird feeder one year. We put it outside the window of our city apartment and stocked it with seed for the pigeons. The city pigeons were either too stupid or too sated by the "pigeon ladies" who feed them to

visit us, it seemed, so our feeder was a failure. It remained outside the window, empty and deserted, for two years.

When we got our country place, we took the bird feeder up with us since we had it and filled it up with leftover bird seed. Being ignorant about birds, I was skeptical that it would attract anything at all.

But it didn't take long for the chickadees to discover the feeder. They were followed by a perky little gray bird with a white breast and tuft of feathers on his head: the Tufted Titmouse. Then came the Juncos, and the Blue Jays—and anyone who has started feeding birds knows what comes next.

We now buy birdseed in 50 pound sacks. Bill has fashioned, whittled, and chiseled half a dozen feeders for our guests. We have platoons of birds that stay to visit all year round or that stop by to rest (and stay for meals) on their flights north and south. Needless to say, we have all become devoted birdwatchers, but the point here is that birds will consume incredible numbers of insect pests for you.

Swallows, for instance, rely almost entirely on insects for food; the purple martin swallow has been called the most useful bird in the garden. (they are said to fancy mosquitos as well). Baltimore orioles eat caterpillars, beetles, ants, grasshoppers, and click beetles; and cuckoos devour hairy caterpillars, beetles, grasshoppers, sawflies, some spiders, tent caterpillars, and crickets. Woodpeckers go after wood boring beetles and fruitwood insects, while towhees

PLANTINGS TO ATTRACT BIRDS TO YOUR GARDEN

SHRUBS AND SMALL TREES
Bayberry
Blackhaw
Buckthorn
Cranberry
Dogwood
Elderberry
Gray Dogwood
Silky Dogwood
Honeysuckle
Inkberry
Japanese Barberry
Autumn Olive
Russian Olive
Pyracantha
Winterberry
Viburnum

VINES
Bittersweet
Greenbrier
Hall's Honeysuckle
Virginia Creeper
Wild Grape

TREES
Alder
Ash
Beech
Birch
Flowering Crab
Flowering Dogwood
Hawthorn
Linden
Maple
Mulberry
Norway Spruce
Oak
Red Cedar
White Spruce
Hemlock
White Pine
Juniper

feast on hibernating beetles and larvae. Meadowlarks will eat some weeds from the lawn as well as bugs. Chickadees, house wrens, and phoebes do a good job of controlling and eating insects. In addition, in the spring, the adult birds must feed themselves and keep their young supplied with insects; at certain times young birds need more than their own weight in food daily.

Recently I came across a garden writer who had compiled a list of "The Best Birds." He then went on to counsel his readers: "Avoid certain other birds." I had to laugh out loud, for there is no way to avoid certain birds unless they wish to avoid you. If you attract any birds at all, they will immediately tell 500 of their closest friends, and you will soon be hosting all of them. I should add that while I think it's marvelous that these birds will eat all sorts of nasty creatures, we do not try to attract them for that reason. It's really because the creatures give us all such pleasure.

If you want to attract birds to your home, what you must do is issue a proper invitation. For a bird, that means a place that provides food, shelter, and, if possible, water.

As to food, you can supply much of their requirements by planting various trees and shrubs that will provide natural food for the birds.

Birds also need supplemental feeding to their regular diet of insects and seeds. In the summer, when there's a lot of natural food available, this isn't a problem. In fact, you should cut down on their rations then or they won't bother

to work for their food.

But in the winter, when food becomes scarce, feeding is essential. Once you start you must continue, for the birds will come to depend upon you for their very lives. Like most people, we feed ours wild bird seed, sunflower seeds (*very* popular), stale bread and baked goods, plus suet. Suet, or beef fat, is a big hit with the insect eaters, like the woodpeckers and chickadees.

Put your bird feeder close to the house (so you can watch the activity) and near some cover—bushes, trees, or shrubs. Bird's don't like to land in an open, unprotected spot; they like to investigate first. By the same token, if you are putting out a bird bath, locate it near some bushes or trees so that a bird with wet feathers can hop or fly easily out of reach of any enemies. Water is a compelling attraction—birds love to play in it, and in areas where it does not rain for weeks on end, water for drinking is essential. I have a neighbor who puts out shallow pans of water near any insect ridden plants. Sometimes she just lets the sprinkler run until puddles from on the ground. The birds, yellow jackets, and praying mantises gather for the water, notice the insect food, and go to work.

Which brings us to predator insects, those that greedily gobble up many garden pests. The friendly and lovely little ladybugs have a greedy appetite for aphids, thrips, tree lice, and eggs and larvae of many other plant destroying insects. Praying mantises (the "walking sticks" of our childhoods) are hard-working, efficient predators. The young eat aphids, flies, and other small, soft bodied insects, while the larger adults consume massive quantities of beetles, caterpillars, grasshoppers, and other damaging garden pests. Two others, possibly not as well known, are lacewing flies (the larvae really go after aphids), and trichogramma wasps (they're especially effective on the larvae of the cabbage worm).

If nature hasn't been upset on your property—that is, if you haven't used a lot of chemical sprays—many of these useful insects will just show up when warm weather comes. If not, you may want to order them from suppliers.

I myself haven't ordered any simply because I haven't need to. The main reason is that we haven't been plagued by infestations of aphids or cabbage worms, so there hasn't been much need to import predators from my point of view. From the point of view of the predators, its just as well because there wouldn'be enough to eat.

However, I understand that what one does with ladybugs is to "plant" them in the garden. They come in convenient cases and can be left in these cases for a few days. Place a little water in the box, and put it in the refrigerator.

To put ladybugs in the garden, dampen the soil and set them out near food (aphids, if you have them).

For praying mantises, you buy the egg cases between November and May. Tie or tape one case to a shrub or tree, at least two or four feet above the ground and near the garden. The cases will survive during the cold months, and the baby mantises will emerge sometime in June or July.

No discussion of natural aids to the gardener would be complete without mentioning the earthworm, a truly remarkable little creature. What they actually do is to swallow the soil, grind it up, mix it with calcium carbonate, pulverize it, send it on through the intestine to be digested by enzymes, and then excrete it. These final earthworm castings contain nitrogen, phosphorus, and potassium, the Big Three nutrients that our vegetables need. And when the earthworm dies, his body adds a good nitrogen fertilizer to the soil.

I have read in several places that earthworms and chemicals don't mix, at least not well. As one botanist put it, "Chemical fertilizers seem to decrease the number of earthworms in the soil, killing them or driving them off; ammonium sulfate is particularly harmful. Many insect sprays also are toxic to earthworms and will cause the population in the soil to dwindle."

So keep that in mind when you are considering what to put into your garden. This same botanist also had this to say about earthworms and soil:

"Earthworms actually are a little finicky about the soil in general. You can't put them in infertile or hard, clayey soils and expect good results. They like rich soil, and if they don't have it, they just take off."

One of the ways you can provide rich soil for your new friends is to start composting. The next chapter will tell you how to do it. ●

Here is a beautiful, prolific plant of golden zucchini at the height of the season. Planting nastursiums near zucchini and other squash plants is supposed to deter the squash borer, which can devastate a plant like this overnight.

Chapter Eight

HOW TO MAKE COMPOST

Homemade soil

One of my aunts lives in Louisiana and enjoys gardening. Like some scientists, she is a genius at miniaturization and has reduced composting to its smallest possible form. Not for her the big, frowzy piles of kitchen peelings, leaves, dirt, and manure. Instead, what she does every day after dinner is to collect the kitchen garbage—there's not much as she lives alone—and go out into the garden. Casting a critical eye around her flower beds, she selects a few plants that look as though they could do with a little something. She then makes a little hole in the ground near the plant, pokes in a a few lettuce leaves and an eggshell or two, and covers it up again. Eventually the stuff rots away and nourishes the soil.

Basically, this is what composting is all about, no matter how alarming the process may sound to the beginner. The purpose of composting plant refuse or debris is so that it will decay. Then it can easily be worked into the soil and will not be unsightly when used in the garden.

You can compost practically any material except meat and animal fats. Leaves, old sod, lawn clippings, straw, eggshells, dog hair clippings (for protein, believe it or not), plant refuse from the garden and kitchen can all go on the compost pile. You can also get leaves from your neighbors who do not use them or from street sweepings. I once met a gardener who lived in a suburban development in Connecticut. He had developed a flourishing truck garden in

This is home-gardening specialist Dick Raymond making a compost pile with autumn leaves. He's got everything he needs—look carefully and you'll see leaves, a hose for watering the pile, and a bucket containing fertilizer to speed up the decomposition. He's already shoveled some dirt over the surface of the leaves in the bin. The bin is a home-made rig, of posts and hardware-store fencing.

a vacant lot across from his house. (He eventually bought the lot). Not only did he get free leaves from his neighbors, but he had them so well trained that they brought the leaves over in sacks and piled them into his garden for him.

When you start to make a compost pile remember it will decay sooner or later, no matter what. The first year we raked up leaves and piled them behind the stone wall. That was about it, since we didn't have much else to add. By early summer the leaves had settled, but they didn't look as though they were doing much in the way of decaying. Bill finally sprinkled some fertilizer on them and covered it over with a layer of dirt, and by the following year we had a passable coarse compost. There are better ways, though.

What most people do is to accumulate the material for the compost heap in some out of the way place in the garden. Fall is a good time to start because you have plenty of natural material to work with—leaves—but there's no reason you can't start in the spring or summer.

You can make a free-standing compost pile right on the ground, which is what we did, or you can fashion a bin of cinder blocks, rough boards, or a wire fence. No matter what you use, allow room for two piles or bins whatever. The reason is that as the compost begins to ripen in the first batch, you can take it out and use it, while adding fresh raw material to the one alongside for use the following year. This is much better than building an ever increasing tower of leaves and grass clippings—a tower in which the wanted compost will always be on the bottom story.

There are also commercial containers for compost, ranging from rather simple wire-mesh fences to a fancy English import that promises that you can "drop garden waste in . . . shovel rich compost out," and an American "composttumbler" that enables the gardener to tumble the stuff around in a drum by cranking a handle rather than turn it over. There are no end to better mousetraps in composting, it seems, but here are a few basic points to keep in mind no matter what method you choose.

Big things take longer to decay than little ones. In other words, the smaller the particle, the faster the decomposition because bacteria can then attack more surface area faster. For this reason many people shred or grind up garden wastes and leaves before adding them to the compost heap. Recently I read an article by a California man who seemed to spend all his waking hours grinding up stuff so he could have the fastest pile in the West, as it were. Well, he had a lot of compost, and he had it in two weeks, but it seemed to be an awful lot of work to me.

By accident I found out a good way to shred the fall leaves. We rake them into a big pile and let the kids make leaf forts and jump around on them for a couple of days. A few days of that treatment shreds leaves beautifully.

Your compost heap will need nitrogen. That is, the bacteria in the compost heap need nitrogen if they are to work efficiently. You can add fresh manure, blood meal, or regular garden fertilizer to supply the nitrogen.

A well-made compost pile will generate heat as it decays. Some of them even steam on cold days. The degree of heat depends upon the size of the pile. If it's not high enough, it will lose heat and bacterial action will slow down. If it's too high, the weight will compress the material in the pile, thus shutting off the air supply to the bacteria. For this reason, most piles seem to be about four to five feet tall.

In addition to nitrogen and air, the bacteria also need moisture. That's why you water it as you go, and why you make a depression in the top to catch rain and snow.

There are many ways of making a compost pile. Here are three of the most popular.

TRADITIONAL COMPOSTING

Spread out a layer of plant refuse or leaves about 6 inches deep and about four feet by four feet. Add ½ pound or 1 cup of regular garden fertilizer, such as 10-10-10 or 5-10-5 to each 10 square feet of surface. Then add one inch of soil and enough water to moisten but not to soak it. Repeat this process until the pile is four to five feet high. Make the top of the pile concave to catch rainwater.

The compost pile will not decay rapidly until the weather warms up in spring and summer. In midsummer, you can speed up the process by forking over the pile with a shovel or manure fork so that the moisture can get to the parts that have remained dry. This is the hard part and this is what has led to English compost makers and American composttumblers,

THE INDORE METHOD

This is a faster method of composting—which is to say that it takes about 12 weeks. It was originally developed by Sir Albert Howard about 50 years ago in India. Sir Albert, a British administrator, was literally surrounded by starving impoverished Indian farmers who had no

Here is a typical bin for making compost—a simple cage made of wire mesh and fastened with twisters. It will keep your leaves and garden debris where you want them. It can also be used as a form to construct many free-standing compost piles—simply slide it up and off when you've filled it to the brim.

Judd Ringer Corp.

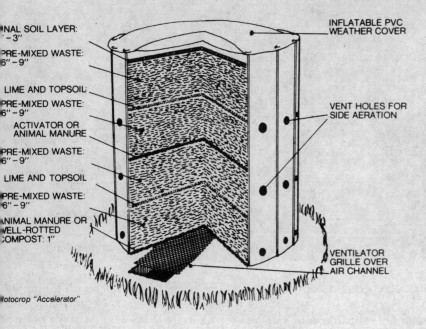

NAL SOIL LAYER:
" – 3"

PRE-MIXED WASTE:
6" – 9"

LIME AND TOPSOIL
PRE-MIXED WASTE:
6" – 9"

ACTIVATOR OR
ANIMAL MANURE

PRE-MIXED WASTE:
6" – 9"

LIME AND TOPSOIL

PRE-MIXED WASTE:
6" – 9"

ANIMAL MANURE OR
WELL-ROTTED
COMPOST: 1"

Rotocrop "Accelerator"

INFLATABLE PVC
WEATHER COVER

VENT HOLES FOR
SIDE AERATION

VENTILATOR
GRILLE OVER
AIR CHANNEL

If you could cut away your compost pile, you would (hopefully) see layers like these. Note how the thick layers of plant and garden debris alternate with thin layers of lime mixed with top soil and "activators," which is simply an extra source of nitrogen added to give the composting microorganisms a head start. An activator can be animal manure, fertilizer, blood or bone meal.

money to buy fertilizer to improve their wasted soil. Their crops were poor, yet they were surrounded by crop wastes and other organic materials that were going to waste. Sir Albert developed a systematic method of composting called the Indore Method because it was developed in that state in India. Here's how you do it.

Strip away the sod so that the compost will lie directly on the bare earth. This will encourage bacteria and earth-earthworms. You can dig a shallow pit to hold the first layer if you want to, but it's not necessary. Spread out a layer of green wilted vegetable stuff or leaves. Cover with two inches of manure, a sprinkling of wood ashes or limestone, and a one inch layer of dirt. Repeat this until the pile is five feet high, watering each layer until the moisture content is like that of a wet sponge. Don't pack it down.

Taper the sides as best you can and make a shallow depression in the top. Cover the whole thing with six inches of hay. Now poke three or four holes down to the ground with a crowbar for ventilation.

Turn the heap three weeks after it's built; five

weeks after the first turn, and four weeks after that. The finished product should be dark and soft with a sweet fragrance.

PLASTIC BAG OR GARBAGE CAN COMPOSTING

If you have racoons or maurading dogs that can tip over or slash open a plastic bag, then put the bag in the garbage can for safety and stability. A can with a tight-fitting lid, incidentally.

If you are just using the bags, use two bags and make a double strength bag by slipping one inside the other. When full, these are very heavy., and you don't want the bottom to fall out.

In either case, put about two inches of soil in the bottom of the bag. Add any kind of kitchen wastes, including vegetable and fruit leftovers, orange peels, coffee grounds, tea leaves, eggshells, and so on. Everything except meat and animal fats. You can also add leaves, grass clippings, and wilted plant debris. Keep it heavy on the wilted green stuff so you'll have a

nice, gooey mixture that will decompose quickly.

Between additions of material, keep the air out by securing the bag with a twist-em. When the container is full, put it out in the hot sun and let it stand covered and untouched for about three weeks. The heat will cook it and it will be ready for use.

Don't peek before then. This method uses anerobic bacteria, the ones that thrive without air, and the decomposing material really stinks. I started one of these in June with some trepidation, but the process worked. My big inspiration was to start filling the bags where I wanted to have the finished compost. When it was done, I just slit them open and dumped the compost into the garden.

The nice thing about this method is that you can use as large or small a container as you have room for. Also once the container or bag is filled, you don't have to do anything at all to it. Nature will carry on from there.

These are but three ways of making compost. It is a fascinating project once you get started on it, and you can also buy it ready-made if you're in a real hurry. Some farmers have developed profitable side-line businesses of selling compost. Some will even ship through the mails.

Probably the best source for further information (which is to say endless information) on the subject of composting is "Organic Gardening and Farming," a monthly magazine published by Rodale Press, Emmaus, Pa., 18049. The

magazine recently ran an article on a man wh[o] uses a bull dozer to turn *his* compost heaps. [I] think I may send it to my aunt to show her wh[at] the opposite of her miniature method *real*[ly] looks like. •

QUESTIONS & ANSWERS ABOUT COMPOSTING

In great gardening countries like Englan[d] and Japan no garden is complete without [a] compost pile, made from garden and kitche[n] wastes to condition and feed the soil. In th[e] United States gardeners still seem to b[e] learning about the benefits of composting and according to the experience of Rotocro[p] (USA) Inc., manufacturers of compost bin[s] there are ten questions most often aske[d] about composting and compost piles.

Here they are, the ten most-often-aske[d] questions about composting:

Does compost have any value as a fe[r]tilizer? Yes, if it is made from materials tha[t] contain essential plant nutrients. Animal ma[nures and green wastes such as grass cli[p]pings and green leaves are a source of *n*[i]trogen; bone meal and rock phosphate are [a] source of *phosphorus* and wood ashes ar[e] an excellent source of *potash*. Compost als[o] *conditions* the soil, improving the moistur[e] holding capacity of sandy soils and breakir[g] up sticky, cold clay soils.

*Rotocrop's Accelerator compost [
makes a ton of rich, fertile comp
within weeks from garden a
kitchen wastes.*

What materials are best for composting? From the house: fruit and vegetable peelings, shredded newspapers, eggshells, coffee grounds, tea bags, wood ashes, cotton and wool rags; from the garden: grass clippings, hedge trimmings, weeds, shredded leaves, animal manures (including dog, cat, rabbit and poultry). Leaves and fibrous weed roots are best shredded with a lawn mower to speed decomposition.

How long does it take to make compost? That depends on the method used and time of year (warm temperatures hasten decomposition). With a compost bin, which prevents waste materials from drying out or becoming waterlogged, it's possible to have useful compost within six weeks.

Is it necessary to add chemicals to a compost pile to help it decompose? No—but what a compost pile often needs is an "activator", which is an additional source of nitrogen to speed decomposition. Nitrogen is obtainable in chemical form but it is also widely available organically. Animal manures, bone meal and fish meal make excellent natural "activators".

Do compost piles attract vermin? Not if the compost is made in a compost bin and the mixture contains no meat scraps. A properly made and well ventilated compost pile becomes too hot, dense, and moist for the comfort of vermin.

Do compost piles have offensive odors? Not if the compost is made in a bin with adequate ventilation. As decomposition occures the mixture will give off a pleasant "yeasty" odor, but it is not offensive.

Do compost heaps need turning? With an exposed compost pile the sides have a tendency to dry out and so turning the heap will ensure thorough decomposition. Turning an exposed heap also aids aeration. With an enclosed bin, ventilation from below and along the sides provides adequate aeration without the need for turning. Also the protection provided by a bin extends fermentation to all areas of the heap.

How can you tell when compost is ready? Well made compost has the appearance of moist, dark, crumbly earth with a pleasant "earthy" odor. It can be shovelled into a wheelbarrow and spread directly onto the garden in spring or fall, or at any time during the growing season as a mulch.

Can compost feed lawns? Yes, and the time to apply it is in fall. Spread it evenly over lawn areas and during winter the compost will work its way into the existing soil. By spring it will be all gone, absorbed into the upper soil surface helping the grass to grow thick and healthy.

Where do I obtain a compost bin? The most widely used compost bin is an Accelerator, made from interlocking green panels with aeration holes in the side and an inflatable cover. For information write: Rotocrop (USA) Inc., 58 Buttonwood Street, New Hope, PA 18938.

Chapter Nine

DIRT-CHEAP

GARDENING

IDEAS

As weekend gardeners, we found that we quickly had to make some choices about what we wanted to do. One of the first questions we had to settle was: how do we want to spend our time? The answer seemed clear enough: doing those things that we found enjoyable, and avoiding the "junk work" of existence—at least as much as possible. But although our goal was clear, the means of attaining it was a little less so.

High on my list of "junk work" is going shopping, whether in supermarkets, department stores, or the big discount garden centers. I always end up buying things I don't need and that I have to cope with once I get home. And while it is possible to put a steak that you didn't really need in the freezer, there is nothing to do with a bargain flat of petunias except to plant them, whether you feel like it or not.

Also, I begrudged the time spent shopping because it took me away from what I really enjoyed—poking about in the garden. Eventually I learned to make only one or two trips to the garden centers in the spring to pick up peat moss, wood chips, some fertilizer, and flats of vegetables and flowers. I went with a list and tried to stick to it as strictly as possible.

While this approach saved me time and money, it also forced me to think of alternative ways of achieving the results I wanted. Black

BRUSH

If you don't want to buy trellis netting for peas, you can prop up the vines by sticking brush into the ground along the rows. The peas will climb right up and over the branches.

EGG CARTONS

Whether of plastic or cardboard, these make good containers for starting seedlings. To use them, first cut the top off the carton, turn it upside down so that it makes a tray for the carton to rest in. If you have a plastic egg carton, poke a few drainage holes in the bottom of each cup with a fine nail or large needle.

Now fill each egg cup with the growing medium of your choice (soil, perlite, spaghnum moss, or a special seed starting mixture.) Make a hole with the pointed end of a pencil and drop a few seeds into each cup. Water well, and cover with plastic until the seeds germinate.

STYROFOAM CUPS

A few trips to the office water cooler or orders from the coffee shop should get you a good supply of free cups to be used for transplanting seedlings when they are big enough (two sets of true leaves).

If you use the cups for tomato seedlings, you will find that they also do a good job as cutworm collars to prevent cutworms from chewing through the stems of the seedlings when they are put out in the garden. To do this, cut the bottom out of the cup and slide the remainder about ¾ of the way up the root ball. Now plant the whole works, and you will have a circular shield around your tender seedlings.

NEWSPAPERS

Newspapers can be very useful in the garden. Not beautiful, but useful.

They make an effective mulch when laid down in the rows between the plants. If you cover them lightly with hay, leaves, or grass clippings they won't look so bad. Weight them down with rocks so they won't blow away.

The best use I have found for them is to begin a new garden where you want to get rid of old and well established weeds and sod. In the spring I put down a thick covering of newspapers—five or six layers—over the area where I wanted our second garden to be. When we had it rototilled that fall, we removed the newspapers and found that the ground under-

plastic, for instance, is highly recommended as a mulch, as I have mentioned before. Since I didn't happen to have any around, I substituted the trimmings from windowshades plus some old shades from our city apartment. When covered with a light blanket of hay, they didn't show at all, and they made an acceptable mulch for one season.

Another really draggy chore we discovered is Going to the Dump. No city sanitationmen up in the country, thank you; we became our very own garbage people, carting our very own trash out to the Town Dump.

Experience quickly taught us that the more we consumed and threw away, the more we would have to Go to the Dump. Wow, was that an incentive to recycle and re-use everything we could think of! We made logs out of newspapers, saved glass jars for putting up pickles and jellies, put as much kitchen garbage as we could into the compost heap, and set out bread crumbs and sandwich crusts for the birds.

However, by avoiding both the shopping center and the dump, we had inadvertently cut ourselves off from the beginnings and ends of the consumer cycle. Being stuck in the middle, we had to do something, so we tried to improvise with what we had on hand. Some of our improvisations you may have tried or heard of, but they are all dirt cheap ideas for gardening.

neath was black, moist, and soft. The papers had effectively smothered the plants beneath, leaving half rotted clumps of roots that were easily dug up by the rototiller.

I have since heard of a woman who put down newspapers in the fall, and when spring came, simply cut some furrows through the papers and planted directly into the ground without bothering to rototill or plow the area.

To enlarge your garden painlessly, make a border of layered newspapers around the edge of the garden each year. Whether you wish to increase it by tabloid or full size sheets, is, of course, a personal decision.

SAVING SEEDS

You can save some seeds from year to year if you have leftovers. Tape the packets securely to keep them fresh and store in a cool, dry place. Here's a chart that tells you how long you can expect your seeds to hold up if stored under proper conditions.

One to two years: Hybrid tomatoes, leeks, onions, parsnips, spinach, corn.

Three years: Beans, carrots, peas.

Four years: Chard, fennel, mustard, pumpkin, beets, pepper, rutabaga, standard tomatoes.

Five years: Brussels sprouts, broccoli, cabbage, cauliflower, cantaloupe, celeraic, celery, Chinese cabbage, collards, cress, cucumber, endive, kale, kohlrabi, lettuce, melons, radishes, squash, turnips.

SHARING SEEDS

To cut your gardening costs, try splitting your seed and seedling orders with a gardening friend or neighbor. You may want only 25 feet of swiss chard instead of the 50 feet you can sow from a packet of seed. A friend can take the other half. Also, you can sometimes get a discount buy buying large packets of seed and sharing the costs. Some garden catalogs offer a free bonus for sending in a quantity order over a certain amount or before a certain date. I am still enjoying a miniature rose bush that I got as a bonus several years ago.

SEED CATALOGS

By now it must be apparent (even to me) that I am a seed catalog freak. They are the very stuff that dreams are made of. They are also very practical. Seed catalogs are a good place to do some comparison shopping, without moving out of your chair, for prices as well as varieties. Many catalogs offer garden seed collec-

tions featuring common popular vegetables at substantial discounts. One grower offers seeds for 12 prize vegetables that "anyone can grow," for $3.95, a savings of $2.30 over his regular catalog price. Of course it's a bargain only if you want to grow everything that's included, which is where sharing with a friend may be of use.

CIGARETTE ASHES

Save the ashes (Ruth Stout, who told me this, saves visitor's cigarette ashes in a little lucite box) and coat your squash seeds with them before you plant. This treatment is supposed to deter the squash borer. I don't know if it works, but the fact is that nicotine is a powerful pest deterrent. Perhaps the plant draws up traces of nicotine all through its system as it's growing.

PLASTIC MILK JUGS

The gallon size jugs are the gardener's best friend. They make terrific individual greenhouses for tender seelings like tomatoes or squash. Because they are translucent, the sun's rays will not burn the seedlings underneath. (At least in my experience, that has been the case). And because they are big, they can remain in place for several weeks until the plant reaches a good size.

We cut the bottoms off the jugs with a serrated kitchen knife. When we are ready to use them in the garden, we press the jug down into the dirt, wriggling it a little to set it solidly in the ground. Then we throw up a little earth along the sides for extra stability. Leave the top off for air circulation. The tomato seedlings we put under their milk jug greenhouses grew twice as fast as those without protection.

Plastic milk jugs also make fair watering cans. Just poke some holes with a hot nail or turkey trusser into the plastic just below the shoulder of the jug and opposite the handle. Make a few holes in the handle so that the water will flow freely. Screw on the top.

WOOD ASHES

Here is another use for wood ashes: as a slug deterrent. Sprinkle them heavily around plants that seem to be slug favorites; the slugs, with their soft bodies, don't like to crawl over the hard, scratchy wood ashes. I should think that coal ashes and clinkers would be even better, but I haven't got any coal to experiment with. •

Sweet corn, fresh from the garden, is a real summertime treat.

Northrup, King, Inc.

Chapter Ten

GROWING A
BETTER GARDEN

TIPS FROM THE EXPERTS

Since I keep extolling the virtues of seed catalogs, I think it's only fair to give you some samples of the fascinating and useful information that can be found in them. (Elsewhere in this book, you'll also find an annotated list of some suppliers of seed catalogs. Nursery catalogs that supply trees, shrubs, and other plants are a different—and equally fascinating—genre altogether.) Many of these companies offer even more detailed instructions on vegetable gardening that you can request when you place your seed order.

THESE VEGETABLES BEST FOR FREEZING

SNAP BEANS—Romano, Top Crop.
SNAP BEANS—(Wax Pod). Butter Wax, Cherokee.
LIMA BEANS—Improved Baby Lima.
CORN—Golden Cross Bantam, Early Sunglow, Iochief.
GREENS—Swiss Chard, Kale, Spinach.
PEAS—Little Marvel, Victory Freezer.
BEETS—Detroit Perfected.
BROCCOLI—Italian Green.
BRUSSEL SPROUTS—Long Island Improved.
CAULIFLOWER—Snowdrift.
SQUASH—Hubbard, Buttercup, Crookneck.
—Gurney Seeds

Harris Seeds

*Brussels Sprouts are an excellent
crop for harvesting in the fall.*

Get the jump on summer and give your vegetable garden an indoor head start. The chart on facing page gives you the particulars. These tomato plants are 6 weeks old and now ready for the great outdoors.

WHEN TO START SEEDS INDOORS

The following chart indicates approximate number of weeks required for popular flowers and vegetables started indoors from seed to develop healthy plants ready for transplanting outdoors in permanent garden location:

KIND	NO. OF WEEKS
Broccoli, Brussels Sprouts, Cabbage, Cauliflower	5-6
Egg Plant, Pepper	8-9
Tomato	6-7
Lettuce	3-4
Vines (cucumber, squash, melons)	3-4
Salvia, Snapdragon, Alyssum	7-8
Geranium	10-12
Impatiens	6-7
Marigold	5-6
Petunia, Pansy	8-9
Zinnia	4-5

—*Gurney Seeds*

EGG PLANT

One oz. produces 2-3000 plants. A packet of hybrid seed should grow 30 plants. Sow egg plant seed early indoors, covering only ¼ in. deep and keep *very warm.* Use a soil heating cable or heat lamps. Start seed in JIFFY PELLETS or transplant seedlings into JIFFY POTS and set out after danger of frost.

The young plants are often injured by insects, but may be protected by light dusting. Dust new growth as it appears. Egg plant does best on rather light rich soil on which tomatoes and peppers have not been grown.

—*Joseph Harris Co.*

FEED YOUR PLANTS

Soils normally cannot provide primary nutrients in the relatively large quantities needed for healthy plant growth. Nitrogen, phosphorous and potash are the primary nutrients needed although secondary trace elements are required. Secondary nutrients are present in sufficient quantities in most good garden soils.

Nitrogen—Promotes rapid growth. Gives healthy, dark green color to plants.

Phosphorous—Stimulates early root formation and growth. Promotes flowering.

Potash—Gives increased vigor and disease resistance. Aids plants in protein production.

Fertilizer—Well rotted organic (animal) fertilizer is high in nitrogen and highly recommended.

Inorganic fertilizers are usually effective if used as directed. Plants need food and should be fed often for best results. You will find a complete line of fertilizers available in this catalog.

—*Gurney Seeds*

GARDEN PLANNING

Whether you're a novice or a "pro", you can grow luscious, vitamin-rich vegetables to enjoy fresh from the garden this summer, and "fresh" from the freezer or canning jar next winter. Burpee "home garden" varieties have been "custom-bred" for perfection in fresh-picked flavor and tenderness, qualities often missing in store bought produce varieties that may be bred for shipping and keeping qualities.

A little planning now will help you get the most from your garden, big or small, with the least effort. Choose the vegetables you like best, and note the number of days to maturity. Many, like radishes and lettuce, are ready to harvest fairly fast, then you can plant another variety like bush beans in the same row. This succession planting keeps all of your space in constant use and productive from spring to fall.

Save room by growing tomatoes "in the air" supported on poles or wire mesh cylinders; cucumbers and pole beans on garden netting, poles, fence or trellis. An added bonus— cleaner, more blemish-free vegetables that are easier to pick.

—*Burpee Seeds*

Burpee Seeds

FAVORITE VEGETABLES FOR A PRODUCTIVE GARDEN
From Spring to Fall — 20 x 25 Feet

1 ft.	Sweet Corn
1 ft.	Kale, after corn is removed
1 ft.	Sweet Corn
2 ft.	Tomato — Large Fruited — 10 staked plants
2 ft.	Tomato — Small Fruited, Cucumbers 4 staked plants on netting
2 ft.	Squash, Zucchini—6 plants Peppers—6 plants
2 ft.	Beans, Bush Snap — 2 successive plantings
1½ ft.	Swiss Chard
1½ ft.	Radishes, follow with Bush Snap Beans
1½ ft.	Spinach, follow with Broccoli
1½ ft.	Parsley — Cabbage, 2 successive plantings
2 ft.	Lettuce, 2 successive plantings
1 ft.	Carrots, 2 successive plantings
1 ft.	Beets, 2 successive plantings
1 ft.	Onions
1½ ft.	Peas, follow with Brussels Sprouts

← —— 20 ft. —— →

Closely spaced rows and successive plantings help you harvest the most from a sunny area 20 x 25 ft. The peas make a mouthwatering feast early, then are removed to make room for Brussels Sprouts. Cucumbers and tomatoes are grown on supports to save space and keep the fruit clean and blemish-free.

MINI VEGETABLE GARDEN
For Maxi Harvest — 6 x 15 Feet

1 ft.	Tomato — Large Fruited — 3 staked plants	
2 ft.	Tomato, Pixie Hybrid — 5 staked plants	Cucumbers on netting or fence — 15 ft.
2 ft.	Zucchini Squash	
2 ft.	Bush Snap Bean	
1½ ft.	Bush Snap Bean — 2nd planting	
1½ ft.	Carrots	
1 ft.	Beets	
1 ft.	Onions	
1 ft.	Lettuce	
1 ft.	Radishes	

← —— 6 ft. —— →

This mini garden in a sunny area yields an amazing amount of tasty, favorite vegetables. The tomatoes and cucumbers are grown on supports "in the air" to save space. Distance between rows is the closest possible for hand cultivation.

73

Burpee Seeds

BURPEE'S HYBRID TOMATOES

For a continuous supply of luscious tomatoes from early summer to frost, plant varieties which ripen in succession.

Each seed of a Hybrid Tomato results from a controlled cross by hand of two distinct parent lines. Hybrids are extremely vigorous, uniform, productive and of a high quality. To produce a maximum crop of best fruit, maintain good fertility and moisture in your soil. Apply a well-balanced garden fertilizer at time of transplanting and again when plants begin to bloom.

HOW TO GROW TOMATOES: 6 to 8 weeks before last expected spring frost sow seeds in sterilized soil. Cover seeds lightly, keep evenly moist. Grow on a sunny windowsill, or 4 to 8 in. below plant lights turned on 12 to 18 hrs. per day. Seeds sprout best at 70°-80°F. (Hybrid varieties especially need plenty of warmth); seedlings grow strongest at 60°-70°F. When they have at least two pair of leaves, transplant to 3 to 4 in. apart. Thin seedlings started in individual containers to one plant each. Transplant outdoors, with as little disturbance to roots as possible, to a sunny location after all danger of frost. Space plants to be grown unstaked in rows at least 3 to 4 ft. apart each way; plants to be trained and pruned; 1½ to 2½ ft. apart in rows 3 to 4 ft. apart. Set dwarf types closer. Determinate varieties having compact plant growth and each stem ends with a blossom cluster are so identified. Tomato leaves are poisonous if eaten.

—Burpee Seeds

THIS CHART SHOWS HOW TO CHANGE YOUR SOIL pH		
Changing pH from	to	Per Square Foot Add
4	5	3 teaspoons Lime
5	6	3 teaspoons Lime
6	7	3 teaspoons Lime
5	4	1 teaspoon Aluminum Sulphate
6	5	1 teaspoon Aluminum Sulphate
7	6	1 teaspoon Aluminum Sulphate

KNOW YOUR SOIL pH

One of the most important factors in growing things begins with properly regulated pH conditions of soil. Soils in the low pH range are called "acid" while soils in the higher pH range are called "alkaline." Certain plants have pH preferences. For instance, the Blue Hydrangeas, Blueberries, Azaleas and Oaks like an acid soil while most plants prefer a slightly alkaline or neutral soil.

To find your soil pH, send a soil sample to one of the universities in your area, or if you want to test your own, you can purchase one of Gurney's Soil Test Kits. It is not always necessary to do this, but helps if you are a superior gardener wanting things perfect.

—*Gurney Seeds*

Northrup, King, Inc.

Burpee Seeds

BEANS

Snap beans—whether green beans or yellow wax beans—are one of our favorite crops. They are easy to grow, and they actually improve the soil by "adding" nitrogen to it. (Peas are the other vegetable that does this). And they are sensational to eat. We like them cooked until they are tender yet crunchy, Nothing can beat the flavor and texture of a freshly picked "crunchy" bean.

They're easy to freeze, and a lot of people can them for winter storage as well.

Plant seeds when all danger of frost is past and the soil is warm. Space your rows 18 to 30 inches apart, and make a furrow about 2 inches deep. Space the beans 2 or 3 inches apart in the row—we use a twig broken to the proper length as a measuring stick—and cover with soil. Tamp the soil down by walking along the row or firming the soil with the back of your rake. This ensures good germination. If you are mulching with hay, pull a light layer of hay right up to the row.

For a continuous supply—and I strongly recommend this so that you don't have bushels and bushels of beans all at once—sow several rows at intervals of a week or 10 days.

If you pick the beans when they are young and really delicious, they will bear more pods. In our first year garden, I followed the advice of a neighbor who said she just left the plants in the ground and they eventually reflowered and produced a second crop. This was true, although the successive crops were poor.

I later heard of another method, which involves some additional work, but which also produces more beans. After the first crop has been picked, strip off the dead foliage and give a heavy booster feeding of liquid fertilizer as a mid-summer snack. The woman who tried this said she harvested second crop that was 60 per cent as large as the first. That's a lot of beans.

eans are a very rewarding
egetable to grow.

Northrup, King, Inc.

You can't get beans like this in the store.

Northrup, King, Inc.

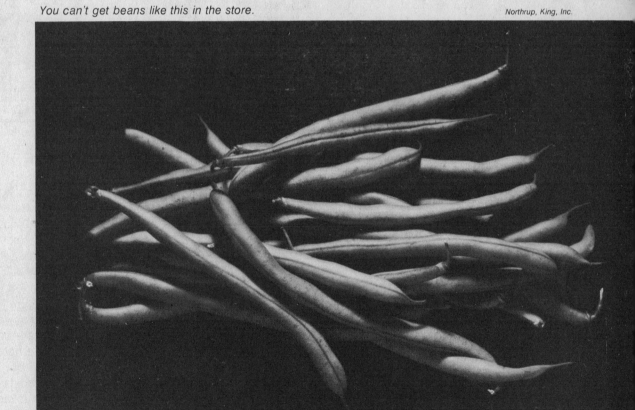

77

BEETS

Beets are a wonderful vegetable for the beginner because you can eat both the roots and the leaves. In fact, we like the tops—the beet greens—better than the beets themselves! You can feast on beet greens as you thin the rows; cook them just as you would spinach.

Planting: Being a root crop, beets really like a well prepared soil, free of lumps and rocks beneath the surface. They prefer a rich, sandy loam, so prepare your garden accordingly. Beets also like a slightly sweet soil, so you can add a lot of your wood ashes here.

Rake out your rows, spacing them 18 to 24 inches apart. Stake the rows and draw a line for the seeds about an inch deep. You'll notice that the seeds are quite large. That's because each seedball, as it's called contains three or more seeds, that produce three or more plants. This is why it's easy to sow too many seeds, and why you must be ruthless later on in thinning. If you don't thin them well, the beet roots will compete for all available moisture and nutrients which will slow down their growth and make them woody. Now cover the planted seeds with one half inch of soil.

Beets are a cool weather crop, so sow seeds as early in the spring as the ground can be worked. For a continuous harvest, sow a few feet every week.

After you have made your final thinning, the beets should stand 2 to 3 inches apart in the rows.

We like the variety Detroit Red for both beets and beet greens, although some people swear by Lutz Green Leaf. Ruby Queen, the only beet ever to win an All-America award, is well worth planting also.

CABBAGE

Cabbage ranks as one of the most important home-garden crops, since it can be grown throughout practically the entire United States.

Cabbage does best in deep, rich loamy soil, and it is a heavy feeder. It likes lots of nitrogen, which is the leaf- or vegetable aiding nutrient, and plenty of potash. Dig in plenty of fertilizer—one expert suggests 5 to 10 poinds of 10-10-10 fertilizer per 100 square feet—at planting time, and plan on side-dressing the crops with additional fertilizer during the growing season. Again use a nitrogen rich fertilizer.

Quality in cabbage is closely associated with quick growth, which means lots of water during dry spells. Never plant cabbage where any of the cabbage family—including broccoli, brussels sprouts, collards, and kohlrabi—was planted the year before.

There are early, mid-season, and late varieties of cabbage. For earliest crop, sow early and midseason cabbage seeds in a hotbed or house; for medium early cabbage, sow in cold frame or open ground seedbed in early spring. For winter use, sow late cabbage in seedbed outdoors when the soil is warm.

Only a few seeds are needed for starting enough plants for the home garden, since 2 or 3 dozen heads of early cabbage are as many as the average family can use. Since one seed packet can produce a hundred plants, this may be a good item for swapping with neighbors! It may also be just as well to buy a flat or two of started seedlings from your local nursery. Set them out 12″ apart in a well prepared bed.

To deter the cabbage worm, Ruth Stout told me that she sprinkles salt on the leaves early in the morning when the dew is still on the plant. An Armenian friend told me that her father used to drizzle weak salt-water solutions on his cabbage plants for the same purpose.

Northrup, King, Inc.

Gurney's

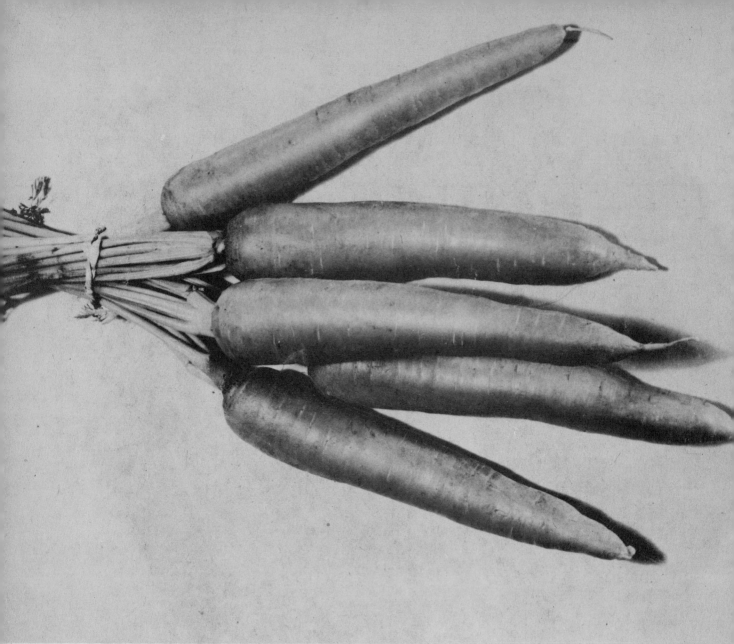

Gurney s

These are Scarlet Nantes Carrots.
Note their uniform shape.

Northrup, King, Inc.

CARROTS

Carrots come in all sizes and shapes these days, so you can pick a variety best suited to your needs and soil requirements. Like all root vegetables, carrots grow best in well worked, stone-free ground but there are sizes and shapes to suit your conditions.

The short, stubby varieties like Little Finger do thrive in shallow or heavy soil, while the long, slender varieties are adapted to deep loamy soils. There are also medium length carrots adapted to the general garden; these include Goldinhart and Royal Chantenay.

Carrots are a cool weather crop that can be seeded as early in the spring as the ground can be worked. To ensure a continuous supply of tender carrots, make succession plantings at intervals of three weeks. They are very fine seeds, so sow them lightly and cover with about ½ inch of soil in rows one foot or more apart. If your soil is heavy, cover them lightly with only ¼ inch of soil.

Carrots also seem to take forever to germinate; for this reason many people like to sow a few radish seeds along the row to mark the row. By the time the carrots are up and growing, you will have eaten the radishes.

When the carrot tops do show, thin the plants to one inch apart. A few weeks later, thin to two inches apart. The tender young carrots are delicious, whether cooked or raw. After your final thinning, the carrots should stand about 10 to 15 plants per foot of row.

CUCUMBERS

This versatile vegetable comes in more sizes and shapes than you can imagine. There are special varieties for pickling, for slicing, and for those who can't tolerate cucumbers (the Burpless variety).

They take little space if you train them up in the air—they'll climb poles, fences and walls if trained properly.

Just a few hills, or a dozen seeds planted and poised to climb a fence or crawl over a wall, will let you pick pecks of cukes all season. Like some squashes, these are a vegetable that produces more the more you pick them. This makes another boon for the gardener. You can pick tiny, finger sized cucumbers if you want; or you can let them get a bit larger for gherkin-sized pickles, or let them grow out for salads or slicing. Watch them carefully; when they begin to ripen, they stretch out fast.

Cucumbers like squash, are tender plants and heavy feeders. Plant your seeds or set out plants out after all danger of frost is past. If you're a little uncertain, cover them with plastic jug greenhouses for protection.

Make a second sowing four or five weeks after the first to furnish cucumbers for later use and pickling.

Cucumbers do best in a very fertile, mellow soil high in decomposed matter from the compost pile. You can also dig in well rotted manure in the planting site. During the summer add side-dressings of commercial fertilizer for booster feedings.

Plant cucumbers in groups 4 to 5 inches apart, placing 8 to 10 seeds in each group. Cover with ½ inch of soil. When plants are 6 to 8 inches high, thin to three or four plants to a group. Or you can sow seeds in rows four to six inches apart against a trellis or fence; later thin plants to stand 12 inches apart in the row.

You can train cucumbers on trellis netting, chicken wire supported by two posts, or against the garden fence. If you are using netting or chicken wire, space the support poles about four feet apart; the laden vines will become very heavy.

Northrup, King, Inc.

Park Seeds

Northrup, King, Inc.

Harris Seeds

LETTUCE

Lettuce is a very easy vegetable for beginners, and can be grown in any home garden. Besides being easy to grow, it is the dieter's friend, tastes delicious, and is chock full of vitamins A and B!

Lettuce is basically a cool weather crop and tends to bolt (go to seed) during the hot months. However, some of the newer varieties can withstand summer heat, so you can manage a season-long supply if you want to. Lettuce, remember, does well in partial shade.

Lettuce likes a rich, well nourished soil, and not too acidy. The USDA recommends fertilizer with a heavy proportion of phosphorus.

You can start lettuce from seedlings started indoors (by you or your local nursery) or from seed. Lettuce will tolerate light frosts, with temperatures dropping to as low as 28° F if the plants have been properly hardened off.

If you want a continuous supply, plan to make successive sowings of different varieties, including some that are resistant to heat.

Sow seeds thinly in rows 14 to 18 inches apart. Cover with about ½ inch of fine soil. Thin seedlings to stand 12 inches apart. For the beginner, leaf and Bibb lettuce are probably the easiest to grow. Personally, I like using seed tapes for lettuce. particularly Parks Master Chef blend, (pictured) which has four different kinds of lettuce on one tape.

Basically, there are four main types of lettuce. Head lettuce, which we usually find in the stores, neatly wrapped in cellophane; butterhead (also known as Boston or bibb Lettuce), loose leaf lettuce, and romaine (also called cos lettuce).

Within these four categories, there are so many varieties of lettuce now that it is impossible to list them all. Your best bet is to consult your seed catalogs, pick a few varieties, and experiment to find the ones that you like the best. You're certain to enjoy eating your experiments.

PEAS

Peas are one of the earliest crops you can plant in the garden, and there is nothing that can beat them freshly picked out of the garden. After the peas are finished, you can follow them with another crop such as carrots or zucchini. These are Lincoln Peas, exceptionally sweet, tender, and flavorful.

Harris Seeds

PEPPERS

These are pretty, very ornamental plants that grow about 2½-3' tall. With their shiny leaves, and white blossoms that turn into glossy green peppers, they make an attractive addition to any part of your garden. I always pick the peppers when they are green, but if you can restrain yourself and leave them on the plant a

Northrup, King, Inc.

while longer, they will ripen and turn red.

Peppers are sensitive to heat and cold, so wait until night temperatures are dependably above 55°. When daytime temperatures exceed 90°, production will slow down markedly; but keep the plants watered, and when the heat wave passes they will return to normal growth.

Peppers benefit from a thick mulch, which keeps the soil cool and moist. They are extremely sensitive to nicotine, which can kill them outright or stunt their growth, so don't smoke around your peppers. Also, be sure to wash your hands if you're a smoker before touching the seedlings.

Peppers should be set out as seedlings. Start them indoors six weeks before the last frost date or buy them locally in flats. Space them about 30" apart in the garden.

RADISHES

Radishes take just twenty to twenty five days to develop during cool weather, and are one of the easiest crops to grow.

You can plant radishes as soon as the ground can be worked; after that, sow more seeds every week or so for a continuous crop. It's best to plant only what you can eat in a

Park Seeds

week or so; then you won't get overloaded with radishes. If you do, you can try radish sandwiches, a great favorite of my next door neighbor. I have heard that you can also cook them; boiled, they are supposed to have a mild, turnip like flavor.

Plant the seeds about 1 inch apart, ½ inch deep. The biggest mistake in growing these is overcrowding. Thin them thoroughly and ruthlessly, and for best flavor, pick them when they're still fairly small and young.

Since radishes are a cool weather crop, don't plant them during the summer. You can squeeze in another crop by planting them about a month before the first frost.

Some popular varieties are Cheery Belle, Champion, and French Breakfast.

SWISS CHARD

This is one of the most versatile, easy and delicious vegetables in the garden. The leaves make an excellent substitute for spinach, meaning that you can use them raw in a chard-mushroom-bacon salad, cooked like greens, or as the flavoring for a delicate quiche. As the leaves get bigger, they develop a thick central rib that can be cooked like asparagus and served with melted butter. So, you see, in one trip down the row, you can pick a salad, a green vegetable for dinner, and a vegetable that could be the basis for a main course for the next day's lunch.

If that weren't enough, swiss chard also holds up during the heat of summer when other leaf vegetables wilt. One planting in spring will last all year (the more you pick from the outside of the head, the more will form on the inside; just don't uproot the whole plant). Swiss chard is quite hardy, so don't be surprised if it is still in your garden up to Christmas.

Chard is actually a kind of a beet that has been developed for its tops rather than its roots. Like beets, each seed cluster contains several seeds, and fairly wide spacing of the seeds facilitates thinning to six or more inches apart.

Only one planting is necessary, and a row 30 to 40 feet long will supply a family generously for the entire summer. We planted half that and found that we couldn't eat it all. The leaves freeze well, like spinach.

Two popular varieties are Lucullus and Rhubarb Chard, which has bright red stalks.

Burpee Seeds

TOMATOES

Without doubt, tomatoes are probably the most popular vegetable in American gardens. Everyone can find a spot to squeeze in a few plants, whether it be a strip of soil along the garage, a bare spot in the foundation plantings, or even a tub on the patio.

Now, with the dazzling varieties of tomatoes, you can find a specimen that's just suited to your needs. You can choose a small cherry tomato, or one that ripens early, or one that sets large fruits. Many varieties now have disease

resistance bred into them; look for the codes VFN, which stands for resistance to the scourges Verticuillium Wilt, Fusarium, and Nematodes. These can be a real plus in areas where these diseases may be a problem.

Home gardeners report two common problems with this vegetable: either the tomatoes have too much leaf growth and not enough ripe fruit, or they have lots of fruit but it takes too long to ripen. In each instance the plant needs phosphorus; use a fertilizer specified for vegetables with a high phosphorus rating.

You can let tomatoes sprawl on the ground, but that takes up an awful lot of room. Most people prefer to stake their tomatoes, and there are many different ways of doing this. Here are some:

Single stake: Drive 6' poles or saplings into the ground, spacing them in a row about 2 feet apart. Plant a single tomato seedling next to each stake, and tie the plant to it as it grows.

Teepee or Tripod stakes: Using 6' stakes, make a teepee with three or four of them and sink the ends into the ground. (tie the top together with string or or light rope). Plant a tomato at the base of each stake, and train the tomatoes up as they grow. This is a much sturdier arrangement than the single stake method, I find.

Japanese Tomato Ring. These are very popular particularly among those with limited garden space, since it requires only a 3 × 3' space for four tomato plants. From wire fencing six feet tall into a 24" to 30" circular column. Inside of this ring, make another ring using 18" high fine wire screening. This section is filled with alternate layers of compost or peat and commercially dried cow manure. Sprinkle each layer generously with an all purpose fertilizer such as 5-10-5.

Set four tomato plants, equally spaced, on the outside of the ring. Train the plants up the wire as growth proceeds. Keep the interior ring well watered, so that the nutrients within will leach out, thus providing plenty of nourishment for the plants.

Tomatoes are a hot weather crop, and should be planted outdoors as seedlings. Plants started from seed indoors must not be set out in spring until all danger of frost is past, and the

Northrup, King, Inc.

...ants must be ripe before the first frost in the ...ll.

To plant the seedlings, loosen the soil for ...ach one to a depth of six inches in a circle ...bout a foot in diameter. Put the plant a little ...eeper in the hole than it had been growing in ...s pot or flat. Set the plant at a 45° angle rather ...an straight up. Tomatoes will root all along ...e stem, and planting them this way will help to develop a wider root system and a stronger plant. .

Tomato seedlings do very well under plastic jug greenhouses.

Since there are so many varieties, it is hard to recommend a single one. We had good luck with Big Early Hybrid, and I have seen others who recommend Supersonic, Better Boy, and Spring Giant.

Burpee Seeds

WINTER SQUASH

The lovely Acorn Squash pictured is one of the most popular varieties of winter squashes—and with good reason. Like their summer squash cousins, they are easy to grow and prolific. If you choose a bush squash, they won't take up too much room—about as much as a summer squash. They are good keepers, and they freeze and can well.

Plant winter squash as you would the summer ones, in a rich, well drained soil after all danger of frost is past. If you are planting one of the "runners," like Blue Hubbard or Buttercup, that will wander all over the place, put them on the edges of your garden. Let them venture out on the lawn or into the bordering weed patch; they'll be perfectly happy and won't be underfoot.

A trick to foil the squash borers with the running varieties of squash is to press the vine down at intervals at a leaf node, and then mound soil over that spot. The vine will send down roots at that point, and if the squash borer attacks the plant at its beginning; well, there will be plenty of roots further on to nourish the outlying fruits.

Leave the winter squash on the vine until the leaves start to wilt and the stems start to shrivel, Cut the plant from the vine with a pruning shears, making sure to leave about 2" of stem attached to the squash. Let them cure in the sun or a warm, dry place for a few days, and then store for the winter. The ideal spot is a cool, dry location if you can find one, and ideally you should store them so that they don't touch one another, which can cause rotting. Check frequently for bad spots.

Acorn squash is a big favorite; we also like Buttercup, which is a much drier, firmer squash and absolutely delicious. The Hubbards are popular in New England especially, and take well to freezing, mashing, and storing.

ZUCCHINI

Zucchini is probably the most popular of the summer squashes, and with good reason. It is easy to grow, unbelievably prolific, and exceptionally versatile as a vegetable. You can eat it raw in salads, make it into soups and breads, use it in casseroles, boil it up as a vegetable, deep fry it as tempura, and stuff it with shrimp or leftovers. Italians like the squash blossoms, dipped in batter and fried in deep fat until they are a crisp, golden brown. Zucchini also makes very good pickles.

Naturally, with all its virtues, my children won't touch it, but that's another story.

Most of the summer squashes now available are bush types that don't take up as much room in the garden as the trailing, vining winter squashes. Still in all, they take up a lot of room, with each plant having a radius of about 4 feet.

Squash is a heavy feeder, so be sure your squash patch is well fertilized. The farmer who rototilled our second garden told us that what they used to do was to dig a fairly good sized hole, and put a few shovels of well rotted manure in the bottom of it. Then they filled in the hole with topsoil, and set the plants or seeds on top.

Squash is a tender crop, a hot weather lover, so plant seeds after all danger of frost is past. Sow six or more seeds 2-3 inches apart in groups or "hills" 3 to 4 inches apart, and later thin to 2 or 3 plants per group. Or you can sow the seeds 6 inches apart in rows 3 to 4 feet apart; thin to 18 inches or more apart in the row.

The more you pick it, the more it will produce. Try to pick the fruits when they are about 6-8 inches long for best flavor. They grow terrifically fast. The small squash you notice today may be the size of a baseball bat tomorrow afternoon.

Squash does very well with a heavy mulch, either black plastic or hay. The mulch also keeps the vegetables clean and free from dirt.

There are many varieties of summer squash—deep green zucchinis, milky-white St. Pat Scallops, and the yellow summer squash. ●

Credits and Acknowledgements

The maps showing first fall frost areas and last expected spring frosts throughout the United States, are reprinted from *Organic Gardening and Farming* magazine, September 1976 and February 1977, published by Rodale Press, Emmaus, PA, 18049. I am also indebted to Rodale Press for permission to reprint "A Companionate Herbal For the Organic Garden."

The list of common garden vegetables, their companions and their antagonists was collected from many sources, most notably the Bio-Dynamic Association and the Herb Society of America.

In addition, I wish to thank the following companies for permission to use photographs and selected information from their catalogs. The information and gardening hints from their catalogs may not be reproduced without the express written permission of the company involved.

W. Atlee Burpee
Gurney Seed and Nursery
Jiffy Products of America
Jos. Harris Co.
Lakeland Nurseries Sales
Northrup, King, Inc.
Park Seeds
Rotocrop (USA) Inc.
Spiegel, Inc.
Sudbury Laboratory, Inc.
TroyBilt Rototillers

I would also like to thank my friends Meg, Jim, Simon and Richard for their continuing encouragement and support.